ISBN 0-8373-6719-0

CS-19 GENERAL APTITUDE AND ABILITIES SERIES

This is your PASSBOOK® for...

Practice and Drill for the Clerk, Typist, and Stenographer Examinations

Test Preparation Study Guide

Questions & Answers

NLC
NATIONAL LEARNING CORPORATION

National Learning Corporation

212 Michael Drive, Syosset, New York 11791

(516) 921-8888
(800) 645-6337
FAX: (516) 921-8743
www.passbooks.com
sales @ passbooks.com
info @ passbooks.com

PRINTED IN THE UNITED STATES OF AMERICA

PASSBOOK®

NOTICE

NATIONAL LEARNING CORPORATION
212 Michael Drive
Syosset, New York 11791

Inquiries re licensing agreements should be addressed to:
The President
National Learning Corporation
212 Michael Drive
Syosset, New York 11791

PASSBOOK SERIES®

THE *PASSBOOK SERIES®* has been created to prepare applicants and candidates for the ultimate academic battlefield – the examination room.

At some time in our lives, each and every one of us may be required to take an examination – for validation, matriculation, admission, qualification, registration, certification, or licensure.

Based on the assumption that every applicant or candidate has met the basic formal educational standards, has taken the required number of courses, and read the necessary texts, the *PASSBOOK SERIES®* furnishes the one special preparation which may assure passing with confidence, instead of failing with insecurity. Examination questions – together with answers – are furnished as the basic vehicle for study so that the mysteries of the examination and its compounding difficulties may be eliminated or diminished by a sure method.

This book is meant to help you pass your examination provided that you qualify and are serious in your objective.

The entire field is reviewed through the huge store of content information which is succinctly presented through a provocative and challenging approach – the question-and-answer method.

A climate of success is established by furnishing the correct answers at the end of each test.

You soon learn to recognize types of questions, forms of questions, and patterns of questioning. You may even begin to anticipate expected outcomes.

You perceive that many questions are repeated or adapted so that you can gain acute insights, which may enable you to score many sure points.

You learn how to confront new questions, or types of questions, and to attack them confidently and work out the correct answers.

You note objectives and emphases, and recognize pitfalls and dangers, so that you may make positive educational adjustments.

Moreover, you are kept fully informed in relation to new concepts, methods, practices, and directions in the field.

You discover that you are actually taking the examination all the time: you are preparing for the examination by "taking" an examination, not by reading extraneous and/or supererogatory textbooks.

In short, this PASSBOOK®, used directedly, should be an important factor in helping you to pass your test.

CLERICAL ABILITIES TEST

EXAMINATION SECTION

CONTENTS

BASIC FUNDAMENTALS OF FILING SCIENCE

CONTENTS

FILING
EXAMINATION SECTION

CONTENTS

Stenographer-Typist Examination

CONTENTS

HOW TO TAKE A TEST

I. YOU MUST PASS AN EXAMINATION

A. WHAT EVERY CANDIDATE SHOULD KNOW

Examination applicants often ask us for help in preparing for the written test. What can I study in advance? What kinds of questions will be asked? How will the test be given? How will the papers be graded?

As an applicant for a civil service examination, you may be wondering about some of these things. Our purpose here is to suggest effective methods of advance study and to describe civil service examinations.

Your chances for success on this examination can be increased if you know how to prepare. Those "pre-examination jitters" can be reduced if you know what to expect. You can even experience an adventure in good citizenship if you know why civil service exams are given.

B. WHY ARE CIVIL SERVICE EXAMINATIONS GIVEN?

Civil service examinations are important to you in two ways. As a citizen, you want public jobs filled by employees who know how to do their work. As a job seeker, you want a fair chance to compete for that job on an equal footing with other candidates. The best-known means of accomplishing this two-fold goal is the competitive examination.

Exams are widely publicized throughout the nation. They may be administered for jobs in federal, state, city, municipal, town or village governments or agencies.

Any citizen may apply, with some limitations, such as the age or residence of applicants. Your experience and education may be reviewed to see whether you meet the requirements for the particular examination. When these requirements exist, they are reasonable and applied consistently to all applicants. Thus, a competitive examination may cause you some uneasiness now, but it is your privilege and safeguard.

C. HOW ARE CIVIL SERVICE EXAMS DEVELOPED?

Examinations are carefully written by trained technicians who are specialists in the field known as "psychological measurement," in consultation with recognized authorities in the field of work that the test will cover. These experts recommend the subject matter areas or skills to be tested; only those knowledges or skills important to your success on the job are included. The most reliable books and source materials available are used as references. Together, the experts and technicians judge the difficulty level of the questions.

Test technicians know how to phrase questions so that the problem is clearly stated. Their ethics do not permit "trick" or "catch" questions. Questions may have been tried out on sample groups, or subjected to statistical analysis, to determine their usefulness.

Written tests are often used in combination with performance tests, ratings of training and experience, and oral interviews. All of these measures combine to form the best-known means of finding the right person for the right job.

II. HOW TO PASS THE WRITTEN TEST

A. NATURE OF THE EXAMINATION

To prepare intelligently for civil service examinations, you should know how they differ from school examinations you have taken. In school you were assigned certain definite pages to read or subjects to cover. The examination questions were quite detailed and usually emphasized memory. Civil service exams, on the other hand, try to discover your present ability to perform the duties of a position, plus your potentiality to learn these duties. In other words, a civil service exam attempts to predict how successful you will be. Questions cover such a broad area that they cannot be as minute and detailed as school exam questions.

In the public service similar kinds of work, or positions, are grouped together in one "class." This process is known as *position-classification.* All the positions in a class are paid according to the salary range for that class. One class title covers all of these positions, and they are all tested by the same examination.

B. FOUR BASIC STEPS

1) Study the announcement

How, then, can you know what subjects to study? Our best answer is: "Learn as much as possible about the class of positions for which you've applied." The exam will test the knowledge, skills and abilities needed to do the work.

Your most valuable source of information about the position you want is the official exam announcement. This announcement lists the training and experience qualifications. Check these standards and apply only if you come reasonably close to meeting them.

The brief description of the position in the examination announcement offers some clues to the subjects which will be tested. Think about the job itself. Review the duties in your mind. Can you perform them, or are there some in which you are rusty? Fill in the blank spots in your preparation.

Many jurisdictions preview the written test in the exam announcement by including a section called "Knowledge and Abilities Required," "Scope of the Examination," or some similar heading. Here you will find out specifically what fields will be tested.

2) Review your own background

Once you learn in general what the position is all about, and what you need to know to do the work, ask yourself which subjects you already know fairly well and which need improvement. You may wonder whether to concentrate on improving your strong areas or on building some background in your fields of weakness. When the announcement has specified "some knowledge" or "considerable knowledge," or has used adjectives like "beginning principles of..." or "advanced ... methods," you can get a clue as to the number and difficulty of questions to be asked in any given field. More questions, and hence broader coverage, would be included for those subjects which are more important in the work. Now weigh your strengths and weaknesses against the job requirements and prepare accordingly.

3) Determine the level of the position

Another way to tell how intensively you should prepare is to understand the level of the job for which you are applying. Is it the entering level? In other words, is this the position in which beginners in a field of work are hired? Or is it an intermediate or advanced level? Sometimes this is indicated by such words as "Junior" or "Senior" in the class title. Other jurisdictions use Roman numerals to designate the level – Clerk I, Clerk II, for example. The word "Supervisor" sometimes appears in the title. If the level is not indicated by the title, check the description of duties. Will you be working under very close supervision, or will you have responsibility for independent decisions in this work?

4) Choose appropriate study materials

Now that you know the subjects to be examined and the relative amount of each subject to be covered, you can choose suitable study materials. For beginning level jobs, or even advanced ones, if you have a pronounced weakness in some aspect of your training, read a modern, standard textbook in that field. Be sure it is up to date and has general coverage. Such books are normally available at your library, and the librarian will be glad to help you locate one. For entry-level positions, questions of appropriate difficulty are chosen – neither highly advanced questions, nor those too simple. Such questions require careful thought but not advanced training.

If the position for which you are applying is technical or advanced, you will read more advanced, specialized material. If you are already familiar with the basic principles of your field, elementary textbooks would waste your time. Concentrate on advanced textbooks and technical periodicals. Think through the concepts and review difficult problems in your field.

These are all general sources. You can get more ideas on your own initiative, following these leads. For example, training manuals and publications of the government agency which employs workers in your field can be useful, particularly for technical and professional positions. A letter or visit to the government department involved may result in more specific study suggestions, and certainly will provide you with a more definite idea of the exact nature of the position you are seeking.

III. KINDS OF TESTS

Tests are used for purposes other than measuring knowledge and ability to perform specified duties. For some positions, it is equally important to test ability to make adjustments to new situations or to profit from training. In others, basic mental abilities not dependent on information are essential. Questions which test these things may not appear as pertinent to the duties of the position as those which test for knowledge and information. Yet they are often highly important parts of a fair examination. For very general questions, it is almost impossible to help you direct your study efforts. What we can do is to point out some of the more common of these general abilities needed in public service positions and describe some typical questions.

1) General information

Broad, general information has been found useful for predicting job success in some kinds of work. This is tested in a variety of ways, from vocabulary lists to questions about current events. Basic background in some field of work, such as sociology or economics, may be sampled in a group of questions. Often these are principles which have become familiar to most persons through exposure rather than through formal training. It is difficult to advise you how to study for these questions; being alert to the world around you is our best suggestion.

2) Verbal ability

An example of an ability needed in many positions is verbal or language ability. Verbal ability is, in brief, the ability to use and understand words. Vocabulary and grammar tests are typical measures of this ability. Reading comprehension or paragraph interpretation questions are common in many kinds of civil service tests. You are given a paragraph of written material and asked to find its central meaning.

3) Numerical ability

Number skills can be tested by the familiar arithmetic problem, by checking paired lists of numbers to see which are alike and which are different, or by interpreting charts and graphs. In the latter test, a graph may be printed in the test booklet which you are asked to use as the basis for answering questions.

4) Observation

A popular test for law-enforcement positions is the observation test. A picture is shown to you for several minutes, then taken away. Questions about the picture test your ability to observe both details and larger elements.

5) Following directions

In many positions in the public service, the employee must be able to carry out written instructions dependably and accurately. You may be given a chart with several columns, each column listing a variety of information. The questions require you to carry out directions involving the information given in the chart.

6) Skills and aptitudes

Performance tests effectively measure some manual skills and aptitudes. When the skill is one in which you are trained, such as typing or shorthand, you can practice. These tests are often very much like those given in business school or high school courses. For many of the other skills and aptitudes, however, no short-time preparation can be made. Skills and abilities natural to you or that you have developed throughout your lifetime are being tested.

Many of the general questions just described provide all the data needed to answer the questions and ask you to use your reasoning ability to find the answers. Your best preparation for these tests, as well as for tests of facts and ideas, is to be at your physical and mental best. You, no doubt, have your own methods of getting into an exam-taking mood and keeping "in shape." The next section lists some ideas on this subject.

IV. KINDS OF QUESTIONS

Only rarely is the "essay" question, which you answer in narrative form, used in civil service tests. Civil service tests are usually of the short-answer type. Full instructions for answering these questions will be given to you at the examination. But in case this is your first experience with short-answer questions and separate answer sheets, here is what you need to know:

1) Multiple-choice Questions

Most popular of the short-answer questions is the "multiple choice" or "best answer" question. It can be used, for example, to test for factual knowledge, ability to solve problems or judgment in meeting situations found at work.

A multiple-choice question is normally one of three types—

- It can begin with an incomplete statement followed by several possible endings. You are to find the one ending which *best* completes the statement, although some of the others may not be entirely wrong.
- It can also be a complete statement in the form of a question which is answered by choosing one of the statements listed.
- It can be in the form of a problem – again you select the best answer.

Here is an example of a multiple-choice question with a discussion which should give you some clues as to the method for choosing the right answer:

When an employee has a complaint about his assignment, the action which will *best* help him overcome his difficulty is to

A. discuss his difficulty with his coworkers
B. take the problem to the head of the organization
C. take the problem to the person who gave him the assignment
D. say nothing to anyone about his complaint

In answering this question, you should study each of the choices to find which is best. Consider choice "A" – Certainly an employee may discuss his complaint with fellow employees, but no change or improvement can result, and the complaint remains unresolved. Choice "B" is a poor choice since the head of the organization probably does not know what assignment you have been given, and taking your problem to him is known as "going over the head" of the supervisor. The supervisor, or person who made the assignment, is the person who can clarify it or correct any injustice. Choice "C" is, therefore, correct. To say nothing, as in choice "D," is unwise. Supervisors have and interest in knowing the problems employees are facing, and the employee is seeking a solution to his problem.

2) True/False Questions

The "true/false" or "right/wrong" form of question is sometimes used. Here a complete statement is given. Your job is to decide whether the statement is right or wrong.

SAMPLE: A person-to-person long-distance telephone call costs less than a station-to-station call to the same city.

This statement is wrong, or false, since person-to-person calls are more expensive.

This is not a complete list of all possible question forms, although most of the others are variations of these common types. You will always get complete directions for answering questions. Be sure you understand *how* to mark your answers – ask questions until you do.

V. RECORDING YOUR ANSWERS

For an examination with very few applicants, you may be told to record your answers in the test booklet itself. Separate answer sheets are much more common. If this separate answer sheet is to be scored by machine – and this is often the case – it is highly important that you mark your answers correctly in order to get credit.

An electric scoring machine is often used in civil service offices because of the speed with which papers can be scored. Machine-scored answer sheets must be marked with a pencil, which will be given to you. This pencil has a high graphite content which responds to the electric scoring machine. As a matter of fact, stray dots may register as answers, so do not let your pencil rest on the answer sheet while you are pondering the correct answer. Also, if your pencil lead breaks or is otherwise defective, ask for another.

Since the answer sheet will be dropped in a slot in the scoring machine, be careful not to bend the corners or get the paper crumpled.

The answer sheet normally has five vertical columns of numbers, with 30 numbers to a column. These numbers correspond to the question numbers in your test booklet. After each number, going across the page are four or five pairs of dotted lines. These short dotted lines have small letters or numbers above them. The first two pairs may also have a "T" or "F" above the letters. This indicates that the first two pairs only are to be used if the questions are of the true-false type. If the questions are multiple choice, disregard the "T" and "F" and pay attention only to the small letters or numbers.

Answer your questions in the manner of the sample that follows:

32. The largest city in the United States is
    - A. Washington, D.C.
    - B. New York City
    - C. Chicago
    - D. Detroit
    - E. San Francisco

1) Choose the answer you think is best. (New York City is the largest, so "B" is correct.)
2) Find the row of dotted lines numbered the same as the question you are answering. (Find row number 32)
3) Find the pair of dotted lines corresponding to the answer. (Find the pair of lines under the mark "B.")
4) Make a solid black mark between the dotted lines.

VI. BEFORE THE TEST

Common sense will help you find procedures to follow to get ready for an examination. Too many of us, however, overlook these sensible measures. Indeed, nervousness and fatigue have been found to be the most serious reasons why applicants fail to do their best on civil service tests. Here is a list of reminders:

- Begin your preparation early – Don't wait until the last minute to go scurrying around for books and materials or to find out what the position is all about.
- Prepare continuously – An hour a night for a week is better than an all-night cram session. This has been definitely established. What is more, a night a

week for a month will return better dividends than crowding your study into a shorter period of time.

- Locate the place of the exam – You have been sent a notice telling you when and where to report for the examination. If the location is in a different town or otherwise unfamiliar to you, it would be well to inquire the best route and learn something about the building.
- Relax the night before the test – Allow your mind to rest. Do not study at all that night. Plan some mild recreation or diversion; then go to bed early and get a good night's sleep.
- Get up early enough to make a leisurely trip to the place for the test – This way unforeseen events, traffic snarls, unfamiliar buildings, etc. will not upset you.
- Dress comfortably – A written test is not a fashion show. You will be known by number and not by name, so wear something comfortable.
- Leave excess paraphernalia at home – Shopping bags and odd bundles will get in your way. You need bring only the items mentioned in the official notice you received; usually everything you need is provided. Do not bring reference books to the exam. They will only confuse those last minutes and be taken away from you when in the test room.
- Arrive somewhat ahead of time – If because of transportation schedules you must get there very early, bring a newspaper or magazine to take your mind off yourself while waiting.
- Locate the examination room – When you have found the proper room, you will be directed to the seat or part of the room where you will sit. Sometimes you are given a sheet of instructions to read while you are waiting. Do not fill out any forms until you are told to do so; just read them and be prepared.
- Relax and prepare to listen to the instructions
- If you have any physical problem that may keep you from doing your best, be sure to tell the test administrator. If you are sick or in poor health, you really cannot do your best on the exam. You can come back and take the test some other time.

VII. AT THE TEST

The day of the test is here and you have the test booklet in your hand. The temptation to get going is very strong. Caution! There is more to success than knowing the right answers. You must know how to identify your papers and understand variations in the type of short-answer question used in this particular examination. Follow these suggestions for maximum results from your efforts:

1) Cooperate with the monitor

The test administrator has a duty to create a situation in which you can be as much at ease as possible. He will give instructions, tell you when to begin, check to see that you are marking your answer sheet correctly, and so on. He is not there to guard you, although he will see that your competitors do not take unfair advantage. He wants to help you do your best.

2) Listen to all instructions

Don't jump the gun! Wait until you understand all directions. In most civil service tests you get more time than you need to answer the questions. So don't be in a hurry.

Read each word of instructions until you clearly understand the meaning. Study the examples, listen to all announcements and follow directions. Ask questions if you do not understand what to do.

3) Identify your papers

Civil service exams are usually identified by number only. You will be assigned a number; you must not put your name on your test papers. Be sure to copy your number correctly. Since more than one exam may be given, copy your exact examination title.

4) Plan your time

Unless you are told that a test is a "speed" or "rate of work" test, speed itself is usually not important. Time enough to answer all the questions will be provided, but this does not mean that you have all day. An overall time limit has been set. Divide the total time (in minutes) by the number of questions to determine the approximate time you have for each question.

5) Do not linger over difficult questions

If you come across a difficult question, mark it with a paper clip (useful to have along) and come back to it when you have been through the booklet. One caution if you do this – be sure to skip a number on your answer sheet as well. Check often to be sure that you have not lost your place and that you are marking in the row numbered the same as the question you are answering.

6) Read the questions

Be sure you know what the question asks! Many capable people are unsuccessful because they failed to *read* the questions correctly.

7) Answer all questions

Unless you have been instructed that a penalty will be deducted for incorrect answers, it is better to guess than to omit a question.

8) Speed tests

It is often better NOT to guess on speed tests. It has been found that on timed tests people are tempted to spend the last few seconds before time is called in marking answers at random – without even reading them – in the hope of picking up a few extra points. To discourage this practice, the instructions may warn you that your score will be "corrected" for guessing. That is, a penalty will be applied. The incorrect answers will be deducted from the correct ones, or some other penalty formula will be used.

9) Review your answers

If you finish before time is called, go back to the questions you guessed or omitted to give them further thought. Review other answers if you have time.

10) Return your test materials

If you are ready to leave before others have finished or time is called, take ALL your materials to the monitor and leave quietly. Never take any test material with you. The monitor can discover whose papers are not complete, and taking a test booklet may be grounds for disqualification.

VIII. EXAMINATION TECHNIQUES

1) Read the general instructions carefully. These are usually printed on the first page of the exam booklet. As a rule, these instructions refer to the timing of the examination; the fact that you should not start work until the signal and must stop work at a signal, etc. If there are any *special* instructions, such as a choice of questions to be answered, make sure that you note this instruction carefully.

2) When you are ready to start work on the examination, that is as soon as the signal has been given, read the instructions to each question booklet, underline any key words or phrases, such as *least*, *best*, *outline*, *describe* and the like. In this way you will tend to answer as requested rather than discover on reviewing your paper that you *listed without describing*, that you selected the *worst* choice rather than the *best* choice, etc.

3) If the examination is of the objective or multiple-choice type – that is, each question will also give a series of possible answers: A, B, C or D, and you are called upon to select the best answer and write the letter next to that answer on your answer paper – it is advisable to start answering each question in turn. There may be anywhere from 50 to 100 such questions in the three or four hours allotted and you can see how much time would be taken if you read through all the questions before beginning to answer any. Furthermore, if you come across a question or group of questions which you know would be difficult to answer, it would undoubtedly affect your handling of all the other questions.

4) If the examination is of the essay type and contains but a few questions, it is a moot point as to whether you should read all the questions before starting to answer any one. Of course, if you are given a choice – say five out of seven and the like – then it is essential to read all the questions so you can eliminate the two that are most difficult. If, however, you are asked to answer all the questions, there may be danger in trying to answer the easiest one first because you may find that you will spend too much time on it. The best technique is to answer the first question, then proceed to the second, etc.

5) Time your answers. Before the exam begins, write down the time it started, then add the time allowed for the examination and write down the time it must be completed, then divide the time available somewhat as follows:
   - If 3-1/2 hours are allowed, that would be 210 minutes. If you have 80 objective-type questions, that would be an average of 2-1/2 minutes per question. Allow yourself no more than 2 minutes per question, or a total of 160 minutes, which will permit about 50 minutes to review.
   - If for the time allotment of 210 minutes there are 7 essay questions to answer, that would average about 30 minutes a question. Give yourself only 25 minutes per question so that you have about 35 minutes to review.

6) The most important instruction is to *read each question* and make sure you know what is wanted. The second most important instruction is to *time yourself properly* so that you answer every question. The third most

important instruction is to *answer every question.* Guess if you have to but include something for each question. Remember that you will receive no credit for a blank and will probably receive some credit if you write something in answer to an essay question. If you guess a letter – say "B" for a multiple-choice question – you may have guessed right. If you leave a blank as an answer to a multiple-choice question, the examiners may respect your feelings but it will not add a point to your score. Some exams may penalize you for wrong answers, so in such cases *only*, you may not want to guess unless you have some basis for your answer.

7) Suggestions

a. Objective-type questions

1. Examine the question booklet for proper sequence of pages and questions
2. Read all instructions carefully
3. Skip any question which seems too difficult; return to it after all other questions have been answered
4. Apportion your time properly; do not spend too much time on any single question or group of questions
5. Note and underline key words – *all, most, fewest, least, best, worst, same, opposite,* etc.
6. Pay particular attention to negatives
7. Note unusual option, e.g., unduly long, short, complex, different or similar in content to the body of the question
8. Observe the use of "hedging" words – *probably, may, most likely,* etc.
9. Make sure that your answer is put next to the same number as the question
10. Do not second-guess unless you have good reason to believe the second answer is definitely more correct
11. Cross out original answer if you decide another answer is more accurate; do not erase until you are ready to hand your paper in
12. Answer all questions; guess unless instructed otherwise
13. Leave time for review

b. Essay questions

1. Read each question carefully
2. Determine exactly what is wanted. Underline key words or phrases.
3. Decide on outline or paragraph answer
4. Include many different points and elements unless asked to develop any one or two points or elements
5. Show impartiality by giving pros and cons unless directed to select one side only
6. Make and write down any assumptions you find necessary to answer the questions
7. Watch your English, grammar, punctuation and choice of words
8. Time your answers; don't crowd material

8) Answering the essay question

Most essay questions can be answered by framing the specific response around several key words or ideas. Here are a few such key words or ideas:

M's: manpower, materials, methods, money, management

P's: purpose, program, policy, plan, procedure, practice, problems, pitfalls, personnel, public relations

a. Six basic steps in handling problems:
    1. Preliminary plan and background development
    2. Collect information, data and facts
    3. Analyze and interpret information, data and facts
    4. Analyze and develop solutions as well as make recommendations
    5. Prepare report and sell recommendations
    6. Install recommendations and follow up effectiveness

b. Pitfalls to avoid
    1. *Taking things for granted* – A statement of the situation does not necessarily imply that each of the elements is necessarily true; for example, a complaint may be invalid and biased so that all that can be taken for granted is that a complaint has been registered
    2. *Considering only one side of a situation* – Wherever possible, indicate several alternatives and then point out the reasons you selected the best one
    3. *Failing to indicate follow up* – Whenever your answer indicates action on your part, make certain that you will take proper follow-up action to see how successful your recommendations, procedures or actions turn out to be
    4. *Taking too long in answering any single question* – Remember to time your answers properly

IX. AFTER THE TEST

Scoring procedures differ in detail among civil service jurisdictions although the general principles are the same. Whether the papers are hand-scored or graded by machine we have described, they are nearly always graded by number. That is, the person who marks the paper knows only the number – never the name – of the applicant. Not until all the papers have been graded will they be matched with names. If other tests, such as training and experience or oral interview ratings have been given, scores will be combined. Different parts of the examination usually have different weights. For example, the written test might count 60 percent of the final grade, and a rating of training and experience 40 percent. In many jurisdictions, veterans will have a certain number of points added to their grades.

After the final grade has been determined, the names are placed in grade order and an eligible list is established. There are various methods for resolving ties between those who get the same final grade – probably the most common is to place first the name of the person whose application was received first. Job offers are made from the eligible list in the order the names appear on it. You will be notified of your grade and your rank as soon as all these computations have been made. This will be done as rapidly as possible.

People who are found to meet the requirements in the announcement are called "eligibles." Their names are put on a list of eligible candidates. An eligible's chances of getting a job depend on how high he stands on this list and how fast agencies are filling jobs from the list.

When a job is to be filled from a list of eligibles, the agency asks for the names of people on the list of eligibles for that job. When the civil service commission receives this request, it sends to the agency the names of the three people highest on this list. Or, if the job to be filled has specialized requirements, the office sends the agency the names of the top three persons who meet these requirements from the general list.

The appointing officer makes a choice from among the three people whose names were sent to him. If the selected person accepts the appointment, the names of the others are put back on the list to be considered for future openings.

That is the rule in hiring from all kinds of eligible lists, whether they are for typist, carpenter, chemist, or something else. For every vacancy, the appointing officer has his choice of any one of the top three eligibles on the list. This explains why the person whose name is on top of the list sometimes does not get an appointment when some of the persons lower on the list do. If the appointing officer chooses the second or third eligible, the No. 1 eligible does not get a job at once, but stays on the list until he is appointed or the list is terminated.

X. HOW TO PASS THE INTERVIEW TEST

The examination for which you applied requires an oral interview test. You have already taken the written test and you are now being called for the interview test – the final part of the formal examination.

You may think that it is not possible to prepare for an interview test and that there are no procedures to follow during an interview. Our purpose is to point out some things you can do in advance that will help you and some good rules to follow and pitfalls to avoid while you are being interviewed.

What is an interview supposed to test?

The written examination is designed to test the technical knowledge and competence of the candidate; the oral is designed to evaluate intangible qualities, not readily measured otherwise, and to establish a list showing the relative fitness of each candidate – as measured against his competitors – for the position sought. Scoring is not on the basis of "right" and "wrong," but on a sliding scale of values ranging from "not passable" to "outstanding." As a matter of fact, it is possible to achieve a relatively low score without a single "incorrect" answer because of evident weakness in the qualities being measured.

Occasionally, an examination may consist entirely of an oral test – either an individual or a group oral. In such cases, information is sought concerning the technical knowledges and abilities of the candidate, since there has been no written examination for this purpose. More commonly, however, an oral test is used to supplement a written examination.

Who conducts interviews?

The composition of oral boards varies among different jurisdictions. In nearly all, a representative of the personnel department serves as chairman. One of the members of the board may be a representative of the department in which the candidate would work. In some cases, "outside experts" are used, and, frequently, a businessman or some other representative of the general public is asked to serve. Labor and management or other special groups may be represented. The aim is to secure the services of experts in the appropriate field.

However the board is composed, it is a good idea (and not at all improper or unethical) to ascertain in advance of the interview who the members are and what groups they represent. When you are introduced to them, you will have some idea of their backgrounds and interests, and at least you will not stutter and stammer over their names.

What should be done before the interview?

While knowledge about the board members is useful and takes some of the surprise element out of the interview, there is other preparation which is more substantive. It *is* possible to prepare for an oral interview – in several ways:

1) Keep a copy of your application and review it carefully before the interview

This may be the only document before the oral board, and the starting point of the interview. Know what education and experience you have listed there, and the sequence and dates of all of it. Sometimes the board will ask you to review the highlights of your experience for them; you should not have to hem and haw doing it.

2) Study the class specification and the examination announcement

Usually, the oral board has one or both of these to guide them. The qualities, characteristics or knowledges required by the position sought are stated in these documents. They offer valuable clues as to the nature of the oral interview. For example, if the job involves supervisory responsibilities, the announcement will usually indicate that knowledge of modern supervisory methods and the qualifications of the candidate as a supervisor will be tested. If so, you can expect such questions, frequently in the form of a hypothetical situation which you are expected to solve. NEVER go into an oral without knowledge of the duties and responsibilities of the job you seek.

3) Think through each qualification required

Try to visualize the kind of questions you would ask if you were a board member. How well could you answer them? Try especially to appraise your own knowledge and background in each area, *measured against the job sought*, and identify any areas in which you are weak. Be critical and realistic – do not flatter yourself.

4) Do some general reading in areas in which you feel you may be weak

For example, if the job involves supervision and your past experience has NOT, some general reading in supervisory methods and practices, particularly in the field of human relations, might be useful. Do NOT study agency procedures or detailed manuals. The oral board will be testing your understanding and capacity, not your memory.

5) Get a good night's sleep and watch your general health and mental attitude

You will want a clear head at the interview. Take care of a cold or any other minor ailment, and of course, no hangovers.

What should be done on the day of the interview?

Now comes the day of the interview itself. Give yourself plenty of time to get there. Plan to arrive somewhat ahead of the scheduled time, particularly if your appointment is in the fore part of the day. If a previous candidate fails to appear, the board might be ready for you a bit early. By early afternoon an oral board is almost invariably behind schedule if there are many candidates, and you may have to wait.

Take along a book or magazine to read, or your application to review, but leave any extraneous material in the waiting room when you go in for your interview. In any event, relax and compose yourself.

The matter of dress is important. The board is forming impressions about you – from your experience, your manners, your attitude, and your appearance. Give your personal appearance careful attention. Dress your best, but not your flashiest. Choose conservative, appropriate clothing, and be sure it is immaculate. This is a business interview, and your appearance should indicate that you regard it as such. Besides, being well groomed and properly dressed will help boost your confidence.

Sooner or later, someone will call your name and escort you into the interview room. *This is it.* From here on you are on your own. It is too late for any more preparation. But remember, you asked for this opportunity to prove your fitness, and you are here because your request was granted.

What happens when you go in?

The usual sequence of events will be as follows: The clerk (who is often the board stenographer) will introduce you to the chairman of the oral board, who will introduce you to the other members of the board. Acknowledge the introductions before you sit down. Do not be surprised if you find a microphone facing you or a stenotypist sitting by. Oral interviews are usually recorded in the event of an appeal or other review.

Usually the chairman of the board will open the interview by reviewing the highlights of your education and work experience from your application – primarily for the benefit of the other members of the board, as well as to get the material into the record. Do not interrupt or comment unless there is an error or significant misinterpretation; if that is the case, do not hesitate. But do not quibble about insignificant matters. Also, he will usually ask you some question about your education, experience or your present job – partly to get you to start talking and to establish the interviewing "rapport." He may start the actual questioning, or turn it over to one of the other members. Frequently, each member undertakes the questioning on a particular area, one in which he is perhaps most competent, so you can expect each member to participate in the examination. Because time is limited, you may also expect some rather abrupt switches in the direction the questioning takes, so do not be upset by it. Normally, a board member will not pursue a single line of questioning unless he discovers a particular strength or weakness.

After each member has participated, the chairman will usually ask whether any member has any further questions, then will ask you if you have anything you wish to add. Unless you are expecting this question, it may floor you. Worse, it may start you off on an extended, extemporaneous speech. The board is not usually seeking more information. The question is principally to offer you a last opportunity to present further qualifications or to indicate that you have nothing to add. So, if you feel that a significant qualification or characteristic has been overlooked, it is proper to point it out in a sentence or so. Do not compliment the board on the thoroughness of their examination – they have been sketchy, and you know it. If you wish, merely say, "No thank you, I have nothing further to add." This is a point where you can "talk yourself out" of a good impression or fail to present an important bit of information. Remember, *you close the interview yourself.*

The chairman will then say, "That is all, Mr. _______, thank you." Do not be startled; the interview is over, and quicker than you think. Thank him, gather your belongings and take your leave. Save your sigh of relief for the other side of the door.

How to put your best foot forward

Throughout this entire process, you may feel that the board individually and collectively is trying to pierce your defenses, seek out your hidden weaknesses and embarrass and confuse you. Actually, this is not true. They are obliged to make an appraisal of your qualifications for the job you are seeking, and they want to see you in your best light. Remember, they must interview all candidates and a non-cooperative candidate may become a failure in spite of their best efforts to bring out his qualifications. Here are 15 suggestions that will help you:

1) Be natural – Keep your attitude confident, not cocky

If you are not confident that you can do the job, do not expect the board to be. Do not apologize for your weaknesses, try to bring out your strong points. The board is interested in a positive, not negative, presentation. Cockiness will antagonize any board member and make him wonder if you are covering up a weakness by a false show of strength.

2) Get comfortable, but don't lounge or sprawl

Sit erectly but not stiffly. A careless posture may lead the board to conclude that you are careless in other things, or at least that you are not impressed by the importance of the occasion. Either conclusion is natural, even if incorrect. Do not fuss with your clothing, a pencil or an ashtray. Your hands may occasionally be useful to emphasize a point; do not let them become a point of distraction.

3) Do not wisecrack or make small talk

This is a serious situation, and your attitude should show that you consider it as such. Further, the time of the board is limited – they do not want to waste it, and neither should you.

4) Do not exaggerate your experience or abilities

In the first place, from information in the application or other interviews and sources, the board may know more about you than you think. Secondly, you probably will not get away with it. An experienced board is rather adept at spotting such a situation, so do not take the chance.

5) If you know a board member, do not make a point of it, yet do not hide it

Certainly you are not fooling him, and probably not the other members of the board. Do not try to take advantage of your acquaintanceship – it will probably do you little good.

6) Do not dominate the interview

Let the board do that. They will give you the clues – do not assume that you have to do all the talking. Realize that the board has a number of questions to ask you, and do not try to take up all the interview time by showing off your extensive knowledge of the answer to the first one.

7) Be attentive

You only have 20 minutes or so, and you should keep your attention at its sharpest throughout. When a member is addressing a problem or question to you, give him your undivided attention. Address your reply principally to him, but do not exclude the other board members.

8) Do not interrupt

A board member may be stating a problem for you to analyze. He will ask you a question when the time comes. Let him state the problem, and wait for the question.

9) Make sure you understand the question

Do not try to answer until you are sure what the question is. If it is not clear, restate it in your own words or ask the board member to clarify it for you. However, do not haggle about minor elements.

10) Reply promptly but not hastily

A common entry on oral board rating sheets is "candidate responded readily," or "candidate hesitated in replies." Respond as promptly and quickly as you can, but do not jump to a hasty, ill-considered answer.

11) Do not be peremptory in your answers

A brief answer is proper – but do not fire your answer back. That is a losing game from your point of view. The board member can probably ask questions much faster than you can answer them.

12) Do not try to create the answer you think the board member wants

He is interested in what kind of mind you have and how it works – not in playing games. Furthermore, he can usually spot this practice and will actually grade you down on it.

13) Do not switch sides in your reply merely to agree with a board member

Frequently, a member will take a contrary position merely to draw you out and to see if you are willing and able to defend your point of view. Do not start a debate, yet do not surrender a good position. If a position is worth taking, it is worth defending.

14) Do not be afraid to admit an error in judgment if you are shown to be wrong

The board knows that you are forced to reply without any opportunity for careful consideration. Your answer may be demonstrably wrong. If so, admit it and get on with the interview.

15) Do not dwell at length on your present job

The opening question may relate to your present assignment. Answer the question but do not go into an extended discussion. You are being examined for a *new* job, not your present one. As a matter of fact, try to phrase ALL your answers in terms of the job for which you are being examined.

Basis of Rating

Probably you will forget most of these "do's" and "don'ts" when you walk into the oral interview room. Even remembering them all will not ensure you a passing grade. Perhaps you did not have the qualifications in the first place. But remembering them will help you to put your best foot forward, without treading on the toes of the board members.

Rumor and popular opinion to the contrary notwithstanding, an oral board wants you to make the best appearance possible. They know you are under pressure – but they also want to see how you respond to it as a guide to what your reaction would be under the pressures of the job you seek. They will be influenced by the degree of poise you display, the personal traits you show and the manner in which you respond.

EXAMINATION SECTION

HOW TO PREPARE FOR THE BASIC SKILL SUBJECTS- ARITHMETIC, VOCABULARY, GRAMMAR, SUPERVISION

Preparing for an examination is an individual process. It depends on the job description, examination announcement, and on your own knowledge and skills. A study of previous examinations and the examination announcement should give you an idea of the kinds of questions you may get; however, developing the various skills in arithmetic, grammar, vocabulary, and supervision needed to answer the questions can be done only by you.

We have listed below some examples relating to these skills which you may need to pass a clerical/supervisory examination. Work out the examples below; if you have difficulty with any one of them, you know that you should definitely go further into the subject. Even if you can do these examples easily, you should review previous examinations for other kinds of problems that may give you difficulty. In any case, you should determine the areas in which you are weak and concentrate your efforts on them. After doing these questions, see whether your answers and methods match the solutions and key answers at the end of this section.

I. ARITHMETIC

1. An office is 12 feet long and 15 feet wide. What will be the cost of covering the floor wall to wall with carpet that sells for $9.00 a square yard?

2. A stenographer spends 13 hours typing, 4 hours taking dictation, and one-fifth of the time filing. What percentage of her time does she spend on miscellaneous duties if she works a 40-hour week?

3. A clerk, who can do $2\frac{1}{4}\%$ of a card-filing job in one hour, works at the rate of 630 cards per hour. How many cards must he file to complete the job?

Were you able to do the above easily? In preparing for an examination which may include arithmetic problems, it is essential that you first review your basic arithmetical operations such as addition, subtraction, multiplication, and division of whole numbers, percentages, fractions, and decimals. A 6th-or 7th-year school text will probably give you all the review you need in these fundamentals. After you review the fundamentals, then apply your knowledge to the kind of questions normally given on the examination for which you are preparing.

II. VOCABULARY

fractious
functional
officious
conducive
congruous
contingent

Did you find these words difficult? If you did, you should do something about improving your vocabulary because these are words that came from previous examinations. Again, it is good to go back to fundamentals. Get into the habit of looking up any word you come across in your reading that you don't know, particularly words that have some relationship to the subject matter of your examination. In examinations for Police Officer, words like duress, indictment, contempt, and deter are used because they have to do, in one form or another, with police action. On the same basis, if you are preparing for a clerical-administrative examination, you should be familiar with the words listed above.

III. GRAMMAR

1. Entering the office, the desk was noticed immediately by the visitor.

2. The office manager estimates that the job, which is to be handled by you and I, will require about two weeks for completion.

3. The supervisor knew that the typist was a quiet, cooperative, efficient, employee.

4. We do not know who you have designated to take charge of the new program.

5. Neither Mr. Smith nor Mr. Jones were able to do their assignment on time.

Did you know what was incorrect in the above sentences? These examples came from previous examinations and reflect common errors in grammar and correct usage. If you had any difficulty with these examples, then a review of basic grammatical and punctuation rules is in order. Look through the grammar questions in the examinations included in this book: you will see that certain errors are repeated in each examination. Stress is placed on such principles as agreement between subject and verb, use of the objective form of the pronoun after a preposition, correct use of who or whom, and the punctuation needed for a restrictive or non-restrictive clause. Your studying, therefore, should be geared to a review of these principles.

IV. SUPERVISION

1. Of the following, the one which is NOT a good rule in disciplining subordinates is for a supervisor to
   A. be as specific as possible in criticizing a subordinate for his faults
   B. allow an extended period to elapse after an error has been committed before reprimanding the offending employee
   C. be sure he has all the facts before reprimanding an employee for an error he has committed
   D. reprimand the employee in private even though the fault was committed publicly

2. "Unity of command" requires that
   A. all units perform the same operation in the same manner
   B. managers comply with established policy at all times
   C. orders be issued through the established line of authority
   D. managers be in general agreement on policy.

3. It is generally best that the greater part of in-service training for the operating employees of an agency in a public jurisdiction be given by
   A. a team of trainers from the central personnel agency of the jurisdiction
   B. training specialists on the staff of the personnel unit of the agency
   C. a team of teachers from the public school system of the jurisdiction
   D. members of the regular supervisory force of the agency

4. Studies of organizations show that formal employee participation in the formulation of work policies before they are put into effect is most likely to result in
   A. a reduction in the length of time required to formulate the policies
   B. an increase in the number of employees affected by the policies
   C. a reduction in the length of time required to implement the policies
   D. an increase in the number of policies formulated within the organization

Did you understand what supervisory principles were involved in the above examples? If not, then a review of supervision is in order. Examinations tend to stress the role of a supervisor as a leader who has understanding of human relations and leadership principles. If you feel a need for a refresher in this area, almost any one of the books on this area listed in our Catalog should be of help to you.

SOLUTIONS/EXPLANATIONS OF ANSWERS

I. ARITHMETIC

1. This problem requires you to know the basic formula for measuring the area of a rectangle (Area= Length x Width) and involves the elementary arithmetical processes of multiplication and division.

First, change the dimensions from feet to yards because the statement indicates that the cost is to be expressed in yards. Since there are 3 feet in a yard, divide the number of feet by 3 to get yards.

$\frac{\text{12 ft. wide}}{\text{3 ft. in a yard}} = \text{4 yards}$ $\qquad \frac{\text{15 ft. long}}{\text{3 ft. in a yard}} = \text{5 yards}$

4 yards x 5 yards = 20 sq. yards needed
x $9.00 cost per square yard
$180.00 cost to cover floor wall to wall

2. This problem requires you to know how to use fractions and how to convert fractions to percentages.

First, find in hours the equivalent of "1/5 of the time filing."

(Multiplying by a fraction) 1/5 x 40 hrs. = time filing = 8
1/5 x 40 hrs. = 8 hrs. filing
13 hrs. typing
4 hrs. dictation
25 hrs. for above duties

40 hrs. work
-25 hrs. accounted for, as above
15 hours for miscellaneous duties

$\frac{15}{40} = 3/8$

(To get % multiply the fraction x 100) $3/8 \times 100 = \frac{300}{8} = 37\frac{1}{2}\%$

3. Rephrase the statement in your mind to read $2\frac{1}{4}\%$ of the total equals 630 cards.

If 630 cards are done in 1 hour, and that represents $2\frac{1}{4}\%$ of the total number of cards, then

$2\frac{1}{4}\%$ of total = 630
or
$\frac{9}{4}\%$ of total = 630

(Change percent to fraction by dividing by 100)

$\frac{9}{400}$ of total = 630

Total = $630 \times \frac{400}{9}$

Total = $\frac{252000}{9}$

Total = 28000 cards

(When we move from one side of the equal sign to the other, the fraction is inverted)

II. VOCABULARY

The improvement of vocabulary requires intensive and extensive study of words and their meanings.

It is impossible to treat this area adequately in this brief overview.

The best preparation is to secure the book on Vocabulary, listed under the heading Basic/General Education, in this Catalog.

III. GRAMMAR

1. This sentence is incorrect because we don't know who entered the office. The sentence, as it stands, has a dangling participle, "entering." It indicates that the desk entered the office, which, obviously, is not so. It would be correct to say "Entering the office, the visitor noticed the desk immediately." Then, there is no question about who entered the office.

2. As you probably noted, the sentence should have read "you and me" following the preposition by instead of "you and I." Prepositions such as by, between, etc., are followed by the objective form of the pronoun - me, him, her, us, and them.

3. This sentence has a punctuation error. No comma is ever placed between the adjective and the noun it modifies. The comma after "efficient" is incorrect. The sentence should read: "The supervisor knew that the typist was a quiet, cooperative, and efficient employee."

4. The sentence should have "whom" instead of "who." What is needed is an object to the verb "designated" and, therefore, "whom," the objective form of the pronoun, is used.

5. The sentence is incorrect because the verb "were" should apply to Mr. Jones, the nearer subject. Following a correlative conjunction such as neither-nor or either-or, the verb should be singular.

IV. SUPERVISION

1. Answer B - Always remember that in answering a question of this type, three of the four choices will probably be GOOD rules to follow in discipline.

   Answers A, C and D ARE good so that leaves B.

   B is NOT a good rule for several reasons:

   1. If you allow an extended period to elapse, both you and he may have *FORGOTTEN* the incident.

   2. He'll probably be making more of the same errors while you are waiting.

   3. Discipline, as a corrective device, is most helpful when the incident or error is fresh in the employee's mind.

   4. The employee may wonder why you waited. He may think you are using this instance as a means of "picking on" him for something else he did or for personal dislike.

2. Answer C - Unity of command by *DEFINITION* means the organizational setup whereby authority and orders follow definite chains or lines of authority. (Look at a typical organization chart.) An important concept associated with this principle is that no member of an organization reports to more than one supervisor.

3. Answer D - Note the wording of the question - "greater part." This question tests your recognition of the principle that one of the supervisor's basic functions is that of employee training and that the regular supervisor in the agency is in the best position to determine what the employee needs to know in order to perform the type, quality, and quantity of work required.

4. Answer C - This answer brings out one of the important forces at work in human relations. People like to participate in preparing plans that may affect them and will, therefore, cooperate more fully in implementing the plans.

EXAMINATION SECTION
TEST 1

DIRECTIONS: Each question or incomplete statement is followed by several suggested answers or completions. Select the one that BEST answers the question or completes the statement. *PRINT THE LETTER OF THE CORRECT ANSWER IN THE SPACE AT THE RIGHT.*

1. The ∧ or caret symbol is a proofreader's mark which means that a 1.___
   A. space should have been left between two words
   B. new paragraph should be indicated
   C. word, phrase, or punctuation mark should be inserted
   D. word that is abbreviated should be spelled out

2. Of the following items, the one which should NOT be omitted from a typed interoffice memorandum is the 2.___
   A. salutation
   B. complementary closing
   C. formal signature
   D. names of those to receive copies

3. A typed rough draft should be double-spaced and should have wide margins PRIMARILY in order to 3.___
   A. save time in making typing corrections
   B. provide room for making insertions and corrections
   C. insure that the report is well-organized
   D. permit faster typing of the draft

4. In tabular reports, when a main heading, secondary heading, and single line of columnar headings are used, a triple space (2 blank lines) would be used after the _____ heading(s). 4.___
   A. main B. secondary
   C. columnar D. main and secondary

5. You have been requested to type a letter to Mr. Brown, a district attorney of a small town. 5.___
   Of the following, the CORRECT salutation to use is Dear
   A. District Attorney Brown: B. Mr. District Attorney:
   C. Mr. Brown: D. Honorable Brown:

6. A form letter that is sent to the public can be made to look more personal in appearance by doing all of the following EXCEPT 6.___
   A. using a meter stamp on the envelope of the letter
   B. having the letter signed with pen and ink
   C. using a good quality of paper for the letter
   D. matching the type used in the letter with that used for *fill-ins*

7. A senior typist is instructing a typist to type a table that contains three column headings. Under each column heading are three items. 7.___
Of the following, which sequence should the senior typist tell the typist to use when typing this table?
Using tabular stops,
   A. first type the headings, and then type the items under them, a column at a time
   B. type each heading with its column of items under it, one column at a time
   C. first type the column of items, then center the headings above them
   D. type the headings and items across the page line by line

8. When a letter is addressed to an agency and a particular person should see it, an *attention line* is used. 8.___
This attention line is USUALLY found
   A. on the envelope only
   B. above the address
   C. below the address
   D. after the agency named in the address

9. The typing technique of *justifying* is used to 9.___
   A. decide how wide margins of different sized letters should be
   B. make all the lines of copy end evenly on the right-hand margin
   C. center headings above columns on tabular typed material
   D. condense the amount of space that is needed to make a manuscript look presentable

10. The date line on a letter is typed correctly when the date is ALL on one line 10.___
   A. with the month written out
   B. with slashes between the numbers
   C. and the month is abbreviated
   D. with a period at the end

11. When considering how wide to make a column when typing a table, the BASIC rule to follow is that the column should be as wide as the longest 11.___
   A. item in the body of the column
   B. heading of all of the columns
   C. item in the body or heading of that column
   D. heading or the longest item in the body of any column on that page

12. When a lengthy quotation is included in a letter or a report, it must be indicated that it is quoted material. 12.___
This may be done by
   A. enclosing the quotation in parentheses
   B. placing an exclamation point at the end of the quotation

C. using the apostrophe marks
D. indenting from the regular margins on the left and right

13. In order to reach the highest rate of speed and the greatest degree of accuracy while typing, it is LEAST important to 13.___
A. maintain good posture
B. keep the hands and arms at a comfortable level
C. strike the keys evenly
D. keep the typing action in the wrists

14. It has been shown that the rate of typing and dictation drops when the secretary is not familiar with the language or topic of the copy. 14.___
A practice that a supervisor might BEST advise to improve the knowledge and therefore increase the rate of typing dictation for such material would be for the secretary to
A. plan a conference with her supervisor to discuss the subject matter
B. read and review correspondence and related technical journals that come into the office
C. recopy or retype previously transcribed material as practice
D. withdraw sample materials from the files to take home for study

15. The one of the following in which the tabulator key is NOT generally used is the 15.___
A. placement of the complimentary close and signature line
B. indentation of paragraphs
C. placement of the date line
D. centering of title headings

16. In order for a business letter to be effective, it is LEAST important that it 16.___
A. say what is meant simply and directly
B. be written in formal language
C. include all information the receiver needs to know
D. be courteously written

17. If you are momentarily called away from your desk while typing a report of a confidential nature, you should cover or turn the copy over and 17.___
A. remove the page being typed from the carriage and file the report
B. ask someone to watch your desk for you
C. roll the cylinder back so that the typed page is not visible
D. spread a folder across the typed page in the carriage to conceal it

18. When typing a table that contains a column of figures and a column of words, the PROPER alignment of the column of figures and the column of words should be an even _____ the column of words. 18.____
    A. right-hand edge for the column of numbers and an even left-hand edge for
    B. right-hand edge for both the column of numbers and
    C. left-hand edge for the column of numbers and an even right-hand edge for
    D. left-hand edge for both the column of numbers and

19. The word *re*, when used in a memorandum, refers to the information that is on the _____ line. 19.____
    A. identification B. subject
    C. attention D. reference

20. Of the following uses of the period, the one which requires NO spacing after it when it is typed is when the period 20.____
    A. follows an abbreviation or an initial
    B. follows a figure or letter at the beginning of a line in a list of items
    C. comes between the initials that make up a single abbreviation
    D. comes at the end of a sentence

21. This mark is a proofreader's mark meaning the word 21.____
    A. is misspelled
    B. should be underlined
    C. should be bold
    D. should be capitalized

22. When typing a report that is double-spaced, the STANDARD recommended practice for indicating the start of new paragraphs is to 22.____
    A. double-space between paragraphs and indent the first word at least five spaces
    B. triple-space between paragraphs and indent the first word at least five spaces
    C. triple-space between paragraphs and type block style at the margin
    D. double-space between paragraphs and type block style at the margin

23. In order to center a heading on a sheet of paper once the center of the paper has been found, the EASIEST and MOST efficient method to use is 23.____
    A. note the scale at each end of the heading to be centered and divide by two
    B. backspace from the center of the paper one space for every two letters and spaces in the heading
    C. arrange the heading around the middle number on the typewriter

D. use a ruler to mark off the amount of space from both sides of the center of the paper that should be taken up by the heading

24. You are about to type a single-spaced letter from a typewritten draft. 24.___
In order to center this letter from top to bottom, your FIRST step should be to
A. determine the number of spaces needed for the top and bottom margins
B. determine the number of spaces needed for the left and right margins
C. count the number of lines, including blank ones, which will be used for the letter
D. subtract from the number of writing lines on the sheet of paper the number of lines that will not be used for the letter

25. When typing a table which lists several amounts of money and the total in a column, the dollar sign should be placed in front of the 25.___
A. first dollar amount *only*
B. total dollar amount *only*
C. first and total dollar amounts *only*
D. all of the amounts of money in the column

26. If a legal document is being prepared and requires necessary information to be typed into blank areas on pre-printed legal forms, the margins for a line of typewritten material should be determined PRIMARILY by 26.___
A. counting the total number of words to be typed
B. the margins set for the pre-printed matter
C. spacing backwards from the right margin rule
D. the estimated width and height of the material to be entered

27. When erasing an error on material you are typing, it is best to move your typewriter carriage to the extreme right or extreme left MAINLY because 27.___
A. this prevents erasure particles from falling into the typewriter
B. it is easier to erase this way instead of at the middle of the typewriter
C. this protects carbon copies from becoming smudged
D. it is easier to erase one letter at a time and not smear words on the original copy

28. Assume that Mr. Frank Foran is an acting official. 28.___
In a letter written to him, the word *acting* would
A. be used with the title in the address and in the salutation
B. not be used with the title in the address
C. be used with the title in the address but not in the salutation
D. not be used with the title in the address or in the salutation

29. Your superior is in conference and has requested that he not be disturbed. 29.___
The ONLY condition under which you should probably disturb him is that
A. a new caller insists he has important business with your superior
B. you are hungry and wish to go to lunch
C. a telegram marked *urgent* is received
D. your superior's wife calls

30. The MAIN reason for keeping a careful record of incoming mail is that 30.___
A. greater speed and accuracy is obtained for answering out-going mail
B. this record is legal evidence
C. it develops the efficiency of the office clerks
D. the information may be useful some day

KEY (CORRECT ANSWERS)

1. C	11. C	21. D
2. D	12. D	22. A
3. B	13. D	23. B
4. B	14. B	24. C
5. C	15. D	25. C
6. A	16. B	26. B
7. D	17. C	27. A
8. C	18. A	28. C
9. B	19. B	29. C
10. A	20. C	30. A

TEST 2

DIRECTIONS: Each question or incomplete statement is followed by several suggested answers or completions. Select the one that BEST answers the question or completes the statement. *PRINT THE LETTER OF THE CORRECT ANSWER IN THE SPACE AT THE RIGHT.*

Questions 1-4.

DIRECTIONS: Questions 1 through 4 are to be answered SOLELY on the basis of the information contained in the passage below.

Modern office methods, geared to ever higher speeds and aimed at ever greater efficiency, are largely the result of the typewriter. The typewriter is a substitute for handwriting; and, in the hands of a skilled typist, not only turns out letters and other documents at least three times faster than a penman can do the work, but turns out the greater volume more uniformly and legibly. With the use of carbon paper and onionskin paper, identical copies can be made at the same time.

The typewriter, besides its effect on the conduct of business and government, has had a very important effect on the position of women. The typewriter has done much to bring women into business and government, and today there are vastly more women than men typists. Many women have used the keys of the typewriter to climb the ladder to responsible managerial positions.

The typewriter, as its name implies, employs type to make an ink impression on paper. For many years, the manual typewriter was the standard machine used. Today, the electric typewriter is dominant, with electronic typewriters, word processors, and computers coming into wider use.

The mechanism of the office manual typewriter includes a set of keys arranged systematically in rows; a semicircular frame of type, connected to the keys by levers; the carriage, or paper carrier; a rubber roller, called a platen, against which the type strikes; and an inked ribbon which makes the impression of the type character when the key strikes it. This machine, once omnipresent is an antique today.

1. The above passage mentions a number of good features of the combination of a skilled typist and a typewriter. Of the following, the feature which is NOT mentioned in the passage is 1.___
   A. speed
   B. uniformity
   C. reliability
   D. legibility

2. According to the above passage, a skilled typist can 2.___
   A. turn out at least five carbon copies of typed matter
   B. type at least three times faster than a penman can write
   C. type more than 80 words a minute
   D. readily move into a managerial position

3. According to the above passage, which of the following is NOT part of the mechanism of a manual typewriter? 3.___
   A. Carbon paper
   B. Paper carrier
   C. Platen
   D. Inked ribbon

4. According to the above passage, the typewriter has helped 4.___
   A. men more than women in business
   B. women in career advancement into management
   C. men and women equally, but women have taken better advantage of it
   D. more women than men, because men generally dislike routine typing work

5. Standard rules for typing spacing have developed through usage. 5.___
   According to these rules, two spaces are left after a(n)
   A. colon
   B. comma
   C. hyphen
   D. opening parenthesis

6. Assume that you have to type the heading CENTERING TYPED HEADINGS on a piece of paper which extends from 0 to 100 on the typewriter scale. You want the heading to be perfectly centered on the paper. 6.___
   In order to find the proper point on the typewriter scale at which to begin typing, you should determine the paper's center point on the typewriter scale and then _____ the number of letters and spaces in the heading.
   A. add
   B. add one-half
   C. subtract
   D. subtract one-half

7. While typing from a rough draft, the practice of reading a line ahead of what you are now typing is considered to be a 7.___
   A. *good* practice; it may prepare your fingers for the words which you will be typing
   B. *good* practice; it may help you to review the subject matter contained in the material
   C. *poor* practice; it may increase your typing speed so that your accuracy is decreased
   D. *poor* practice; it may cause you to lose your concentration and make errors in the words you are presently typing

8. Assume that you are transcribing a letter and you are not sure how to divide a word at the end of a line you are typing. 8.___
   The BEST way to determine where to divide the word is by

A. asking your supervisor
B. asking the person who dictated the letter
C. checking with other stenographers
D. looking up the word in a dictionary

9. When taking proper care of a typewriter, it is NOT a desirable action to 9.___
A. clean the feed rolls with a cloth
B. dust the exterior surface of the machine
C. oil the rubber parts of the machine
D. use a type-cleaning brush to clean the keys

10. Of the following, the LEAST desirable action to take when typing a rough draft of a report is to 10.___
A. cross out typing errors instead of erasing them
B. double or triple space between lines
C. provide large margins on all sides of the typing paper
D. use letterhead or onionskin paper

11. The *date line* of every business letter should indicate the month, the day of the month, and the year. 11.___
The MOST common practice when typing a *date line* is to type it as
A. Jan. 12, 2006
B. January 12, 2006
C. 1-12-06
D. 1/12/06

Questions 12-16.

DIRECTIONS: Questions 12 through 16 are to be answered SOLELY on the basis of the information provided in the following passage.

A written report is a communication of information from one person to another. It is an account of some matter especially investigated, however routine that matter may be. The ultimate basis of any good written report is facts, which become known through observation and verification. Good written reports may seem to be no more than general ideas and opinions. However, in such cases, the facts leading to these opinions were gathered, verified, and reported earlier, and the opinions are dependent upon these facts. Good style, proper form, and emphasis cannot make a good written report out of unreliable information and bad judgment; but on the other hand, solid investigation and brilliant thinking are not likely to become very useful until they are effectively communicated to others. If a person's work calls for written reports, then his work is often no better than his written reports.

12. Based on the information in the above passage, it can be concluded that opinions expressed in a report should be 12.___
A. based on facts which are gathered and reported
B. emphasized repeatedly when they result from a special investigation
C. kept to a minimum
D. separated from the body of the report

13. In the above passage, the one of the following which is mentioned as a way of establishing facts is 13.___
A. authority B. communication
C. reporting D. verification

14. According to the above passage, the characteristic shared by ALL written reports is that they are 14.___
A. accounts of routine matters
B. transmissions of information
C. reliable and logical
D. written in proper form

15. Which of the following conclusions can LOGICALLY be drawn from the information given in the above passage? 15.___
A. Brilliant thinking can make up for unreliable information in a report.
B. One method of judging an individual's work is the quality of the written reports he is required to submit.
C. Proper form and emphasis can make a good report out of unreliable information.
D. Good written reports that seem to be no more than general ideas should be rewritten.

16. Which of the following suggested titles would be MOST appropriate for this passage? 16.___
A. GATHERING AND ORGANIZING FACTS
B. TECHNIQUES OF OBSERVATION
C. NATURE AND PURPOSE OF REPORTS
D. REPORTS AND OPINIONS: DIFFERENCES AND SIMILARITIES

Questions 17-25.

DIRECTIONS: Each of Questions 17 through 25 consists of a sentence which may or may not be an example of good English usage. Examine each sentence, considering grammar, punctuation, spelling, capitalization, and awkwardness. Then choose the correct statement about it from the four choices below it. If the English usage in the sentence given is better than any of the changes suggested in Choices B, C, or D, pick choice A. Do NOT pick a choice that will change the meaning of the sentence.

17. We attended a staff conference on Wednesday the new safety and fire rules were discussed. 17.___
A. This is an example of acceptable writing.
B. The words *safety*, *fire*, and *rules* should begin with capital letters.
C. There should be a comma after the word *Wednesday*.
D. There should be a period after the word *Wednesday*, and the word *the* should begin with a capital letter.

18. Neither the dictionary or the telephone directory could be found in the office library. 18.___
   A. This is an example of acceptable writing.
   B. The word *or* should be changed to *nor*.
   C. The word *library* should be spelled *libery*.
   D. The word *neither* should be changed to *either*.

19. The report would have been typed correctly if the typist could read the draft. 19.___
   A. This is an example of acceptable writing.
   B. The word *would* should be removed.
   C. The word *have* should be inserted after the word *could*.
   D. The word *correctly* should be changed to *correct*.

20. The supervisor brought the reports and forms to an employees desk. 20.___
   A. This is an example of acceptable writing.
   B. The word *brought* should be changed to *took*.
   C. There should be a comma after the word *reports* and a comma after the word *forms*.
   D. The word *employees* should be spelled *employee's*.

21. It's important for all the office personnel to submit their vacation schedules on time. 21.___
   A. This is an example of acceptable writing.
   B. The word *It's* should be spelled *Its*.
   C. The word *their* should be spelled *they're*.
   D. The word *personnel* should be spelled *personal*.

22. The supervisor wants that all staff members report to the office at 9:00 A.M. 22.___
   A. This is an example of acceptable writing.
   B. The word *that* should be removed and the word *to* should be inserted after the word *members*.
   C. There should be a comma after the word *wants* and a comma after the word *office*.
   D. The word *wants* should be changed to *want* and the word *shall* should be inserted after the word *members*.

23. Every morning the clerk opens the office mail and distributes it. 23.___
   A. This is an example of acceptable writing.
   B. The word *opens* should be changed to *open*.
   C. The word *mail* should be changed to *letters*.
   D. The word *it* should be changed to *them*.

24. The secretary typed more fast on an electric typewriter than on a manual typewriter. 24.___
   A. This is an example of acceptable writing.
   B. The words *more fast* should be changed to *faster*.
   C. There should be a comma after the words *electric typewriter*.
   D. The word *than* should be changed to *then*.

25. The new stenographer needed a desk a typewriter, a chair and a blotter. 25.___
   A. This is an example of acceptable writing.
   B. The word *blotter* should be spelled *blodder*.
   C. The word *stenographer* should begin with a capital letter.
   D. There should be a comma after the word *desk*.

KEY (CORRECT ANSWERS)

1. C
2. B
3. A
4. B
5. A

6. D
7. D
8. D
9. C
10. D

11. B
12. A
13. D
14. B
15. B

16. C
17. D
18. B
19. C
20. D

21. A
22. B
23. A
24. B
25. D

EXAMINATION SECTION

DIRECTIONS: Each question or incomplete statement is followed by several suggested answers or completions. Select the one that BEST answers the question or completes the statement. *PRINT THE LETTER OF THE CORRECT ANSWER IN THE SPACE AT THE RIGHT.*

Questions 1-10.

WORD MEANING

DIRECTIONS: Each question from 1 to 10 contains a word in capitals followed by four suggested meanings of the word. For each question, choose the best meaning. *PRINT THE LETTER OF THE CORRECT ANSWER IN THE SPACE AT THE RIGHT.*

1. ACCURATE 1.___
   A. correct B. useful C. afraid D. careless

2. ALTER 2.___
   A. copy B. change C. report D. agree

3. DOCUMENT 3.___
   A. outline B. agreement C. blueprint D. record

4. INDICATE 4.___
   A. listen B. show C. guess D. try

5. INVENTORY 5.___
   A. custom B. discovery C. warning D. list

6. ISSUE 6.___
   A. annoy B. use up C. give out D. gain

7. NOTIFY 7.___
   A. inform B. promise C. approve D. strengthen

8. ROUTINE 8.___
   A. path B. mistake C. habit D. journey

9. TERMINATE 9.___
   A. rest B. start C. deny D. end

10. TRANSMIT 10.___
    A. put in B. send C. stop D. go across

Questions 11-15.

READING COMPREHENSION

DIRECTIONS: Questions 11 through 15 test how well you understand what you read. It will be necessary for you to read carefully because your answers to these questions should be based ONLY on the information given in the following paragraphs.

The recipient gains an impression of a typewritten letter before he begins to read the message. Factors which provide for a good first impression include margins and spacing that are visually pleasing, formal parts of the letter which are correctly placed according to the style of the letter, copy which is free of obvious erasures and over-strikes, and transcript that is even and clear. The problem for the typist is that of how to produce that first, positive impression of her work.

There are several general rules which a typist can follow when she wishes to prepare a properly spaced letter on a sheet of letter-head. Ordinarily, the width of a letter should not be less than four inches nor more than six inches. The side margins should also have a desirable relation to the bottom margin and the space between the letterhead and the body of the letter. Usually the most appealing arrangement is when the side margins are even and the bottom margin is slightly wider than the side margins. In some offices, however, standard line length is used for all business letters, and the secretary then varies the spacing between the date line and the inside address according to the length of the letter.

11. The BEST title for the above paragraphs would be: 11.___
   A. Writing Office Letters
   B. Making Good First Impressions
   C. Judging Well-Typed Letters
   D. Good Placing and Spacing for Office Letters

12. According to the above paragraphs, which of the following might be considered the way in which people very quickly judge the quality of work which has been typed? By 12.___
   A. measuring the margins to see if they are correct
   B. looking at the spacing and cleanliness of the typescript
   C. scanning the body of the letter for meaning
   D. reading the date line and address for errors

13. What, according to the above paragraphs, would be definitely UNDESIRABLE as the average line length of a typed letter? 13.___
   A. 4"   B. 5"   C. 6"   D. 7"

14. According to the above paragraphs, when the line length is kept standard, the secretary 14.___
   A. does not have to vary the spacing at all since this also is standard
   B. adjusts the spacing between the date line and inside address for different lengths of letters

C. uses the longest line as a guideline for spacing between the date line and inside address
D. varies the number of spaces between the lines

15. According to the above paragraphs, side margins are MOST pleasing when they 15.___
A. are even and somewhat smaller than the bottom margin
B. are slightly wider than the bottom margin
C. vary with the length of the letter
D. are figured independently from the letterhead and the body of the letter

Questions 16-20.

CODING

DIRECTIONS:

Name of Applicant	H	A	N	G	S	B	R	U	K	E
Test Code	c	o	m	p	l	e	x	i	t	y
File Number	0	1	2	3	4	5	6	7	8	9

Assume that each of the above capital letters is the first letter of the name of an Applicant, that the small letter directly beneath each capital letter is the test code for the Applicant, and that the number directly beneath each code letter is the file number for the Applicant.

In each of the following Questions 16 through 20, the test code letters and the file numbers in Columns 2 and 3 should correspond to the capital letters in Column 1. For each question, look at each column carefully and mark your answer as follows:

If there is an error only in Column 2, mark your answer A.
If there is an error only in Column 3, mark your answer B.
If there is an error in both Columns 2 and 3, mark your answer C.
If both Columns 2 and 3 are correct, mark your answer D.

The following sample question is given to help you understand the procedure.

SAMPLE QUESTION

Column 1	Column 2	Column 3
AKEHN	otyci	18902

In Column 2, the final test code letter *i* should be *m*. Column 3 is correctly coded to Column 1. Since there is an error only in Column 2, the answer is A.

	Column 1	Column 2	Column 3	
16.	NEKKU	mytti	29987	16.___
17.	KRAEB	txyle	86095	17.___
18.	ENAUK	ymoit	92178	18.___
19.	REANA	xeomo	69121	19.___
20.	EKHSE	ytcxy	97049	20.___

Questions 21-30.

ARITHMETICAL REASONING

21. If a secretary answered 28 phone calls and typed the addresses for 112 credit statements in one morning, what is the ratio of phone calls answered to credit statements typed for that period of time? 21.___
    A. 1:4 B. 1:7 C. 2:3 D. 3:5

22. According to a suggested filing system, no more than 10 folders should be filed behind any one file guide and from 15 to 25 file guides should be used in each file drawer for easy finding and filing. 22.___
    The maximum number of folders that a five-drawer file cabinet can hold to allow easy finding and filing is
    A. 550 B. 750 C. 1,100 D. 1,250

23. An employee had a starting salary of $25,804. He received a salary increase at the end of each year, and at the end of the seventh year his salary was $33,476. 23.___
    What was his average annual increase in salary over these seven years?
    A. $1,020 B. $1,076 C. $1,096 D. $1,144

24. The 55 typists and 28 senior clerks in a certain city agency were paid a total of $1,943,200 in salaries last year. 24.___
    If the average annual salary of a typist was $22,400 the average annual salary of a senior clerk was
    A. $25,400 B. $26,600 C. $26,800 D. $27,000

25. A typist has been given a three page report to type. She has finished typing the first two pages. The first page has 283 words, and the second page has 366 words. 25.___
    If the total report consists of 954 words, how many words will she have to type on the third page of the report?
    A. 202 B. 287 C. 305 D. 313

26. In one day, Clerk A processed 30% more forms than Clerk B, and Clerk C processed $1\frac{1}{4}$ times as many forms as Clerk A. If Clerk B processed 40 forms, how many more forms were processed by Clerk C than Clerk B? 26.___
    A. 12 B. 13 C. 21 D. 25

27. A clerk who earns a gross salary of $452 every two weeks has the following deductions taken from her paycheck: 15% for City, State, Federal taxes; $2\frac{1}{2}$% for Social Security; $1.30 for health insurance; and $6.00 for union dues. The amount of her take-home pay is 27.____
   A. $256.20 B. $312.40 C. $331.60 D. $365.60

28. In 2005, a city agency spent $200 to buy pencils at a cost of 50¢ a dozen. If the agency used 3/4 of these pencils in 2005 and used the same number of pencils in 2006, how many more pencils did it have to buy to have enough pencils for all of 2006? 28.____
   A. 1,200 B. 2,400 C. 3,600 D. 4,800

29. A clerk who worked in Agency X earned the following salaries: $20,140 the first year, $21,000 the second year, and $21,920 the third year. Another clerk who worked in Agency Y for three years earned $21,100 a year for two years and $21,448 the third year. The difference between the average salaries received by both clerks over a three-year period is 29.____
   A. $196 B. $204 C. $348 D. $564

30. An employee who works over 40 hours in any week receives overtime payment for the extra hours at time and one-half ($1\frac{1}{2}$ times) his hourly rate of pay. An employee who earns $6.80 an hour works a total of 45 hours during a certain week. His total pay for that week would be 30.____
   A. $282.20 B. $306.00 C. $323.00 D. $406.00

Questions 31-35.

RELATED INFORMATION

31. To tell a newly-employed clerk to fill a top drawer of a four-drawer cabinet with heavy folders which will be often used and to keep lower drawers only partly filled is 31.____
   A. *good*, because a tall person would have to bend unnecessarily if he had to use a lower drawer
   B. *bad*, because the file cabinet may tip over when the top drawer is opened
   C. *good*, because it is the most easily reachable drawer for the average person
   D. *bad*, because a person bending down at another drawer may accidentally bang his head on the bottom of the drawer when he straightens up

32. If a senior typist or senior clerk has requisitioned a *ream* of paper in order to duplicate a single page office announcement, how many announcements can be printed from the one package of paper? 32.____
   A. 200 B. 500 C. 700 D. 1,000

33. Your supervisor has asked you to locate a telephone number for an attorney named Jones, whose office is located at 311 Broadway, and whose name is not already listed in your files. 33.___
The BEST method for finding the number would be for you to
   A. call the information operator and have her get it for you
   B. look in the alphabetical directory (white pages) under the name Jones at 311 Broadway
   C. refer to the heading Attorney in the yellow pages for the name Jones at 311 Broadway
   D. ask your supervisor who referred her to Mr. Jones, then call that person for the number

34. An example of material that should NOT be sent by first class mail is a 34.___
   A. email copy of a letter B. post card
   C. business reply card D. large catalogue

35. In the operations of a government agency, a voucher is ORDINARILY used to 35.___
   A. refer someone to the agency for a position or assignment
   B. certify that an agency's records of financial transactions are accurate
   C. order payment from agency funds of a stated amount to an individual
   D. enter a statement of official opinion in the records of the agency

Questions 36-40.

ENGLISH USAGE

DIRECTIONS: Each question from 36 through 40 contains a sentence. Read each sentence carefully to decide whether it is correct. Then, in the space at the right, mark your answer:

(A) if the sentence is incorrect because of bad grammar or sentence structure
(B) if the sentence is incorrect because of bad punctuation
(C) if the sentence is incorrect because of bad capitalization
(D) if the sentence is correct

Each incorrect sentence has only one type of error. Consider a sentence correct if it has no errors, although there may be other correct ways of saying the same thing.

SAMPLE QUESTION I: One of our clerks were promoted yesterday.

The subject of this sentence is *one*, so the verb should be *was promoted* instead of *were promoted*. Since the sentence is incorrect because of bad grammar, the answer to Sample Question I is (A).

SAMPLE QUESTION II: Between you and me, I would prefer not going there.

Since this sentence is correct, the answer to Sample Question II is (D).

36. The National alliance of Businessmen is trying to persuade private businesses to hire youth in the summertime. 36.___

37. The supervisor who is on vacation, is in charge of processing vouchers. 37.___

38. The activity of the committee at its conferences is always stimulating. 38.___

39. After checking the addresses again, the letters went to the mailroom. 39.___

40. The director, as well as the employees, are interested in sharing the dividends. 40.___

Questions 41-45.

FILING

DIRECTIONS: Each question from 41 through 45 contains four names. For each question, choose the name that should be FIRST if the four names are to be arranged in alphabetical order in accordance with the Rules for Alphabetical Filing given below. Read these rules carefully. Then, for each question, indicate in the space at the right the letter before the name that should be FIRST in alphabetical order.

RULES FOR ALPHABETICAL FILING

Names of People

(1) The names of people are filed in strict alphabetical order, first according to the last name, then according to first name or initial, and finally according to middle name or initial. FOR EXAMPLE: George Allen comes before Edward Bell, and Leonard P. Reston comes before Lucille B. Reston.

(2) When last names are the same, FOR EXAMPLE, A. Green and Agnes Green, the one with the initial comes before the one with the name written out when the first initials are identical.

(3) When first and last names are alike and the middle name is given, FOR EXAMPLE, John David Doe and John Devoe Doe, the names should be filed in the alphabetical order of the middle names.

(4) When first and last names are the same, a name without a middle initial comes before one with a middle name or initial. FOR EXAMPLE, John Doe comes before both John A. Doe and John Alan Doe.

(5) *When first and last names are the same, a name with a middle initial comes before one with a middle name beginning with the same initial. FOR EXAMPLE: Jack R. Hertz comes before Jack Richard Hertz.*

(6) *Prefixes such as De, O', Mac, Mc, and Van are filed as written and are treated as part of the names to which they are connected. FOR EXAMPLE: Robert O'Dea is filed before David Olsen.*

(7) *Abbreviated names are treated as if they were spelled out. FOR EXAMPLE: Chas. is filed as Charles and Thos. is filed as Thomas.*

(8) *Titles and designations such as Dr., Mr., and Prof. are disregarded in filing.*

Names of Organizations

(1) *The names of business organizations are filed according to the order in which each word in the name appears. When an organization name bears the name of a person, it is filed according to the rules for filing names of people as given above. FOR EXAMPLE: William Smith Service Co. comes before Television Distributors, Inc.*

(2) *Where bureau, board, office, or department appears as the first part of the title of a governmental agency, that agency should be filed under the word in the title expressing the chief function of the agency. FOR EXAMPLE: Bureau of the Budget would be filed as if written Budget, (Bureau of the). The Department of Personnel would be filed as if written Personnel, (Department of).*

(3) *When the following words are part of an organization, they are disregarded: the, of, and.*

(4) *When there are numbers in a name, they are treated as if they were spelled out. FOR EXAMPLE: 10th Street Bootery is filed as Tenth Street Bootery.*

SAMPLE QUESTION:

A.	Jane Earl	(2)
B.	James A. Earle	(4)
C.	James Earl	(1)
D.	J. Earle	(3)

The numbers in parentheses show the proper alphabetical order in which these names should be filed. Since the name that should be filed FIRST is James Earl, the answer to the Sample Question is (C).

41. A. Majorca Leather Goods 41.___
B. Robert Maiorca and Sons
C. Maintenance Management Corp.
D. Majestic Carpet Mills

42. A. Municipal Telephone Service 42.___
B. Municipal Reference Library
C. Municipal Credit Union
D. Municipal Broadcasting System

43. A. Robert B. Pierce B. R. Bruce Pierce 43.___
C. Ronald Pierce D. Robert Bruce Pierce

44. A. Four Seasons Sports Club B. 14th. St. Shopping Center 44.___
C. Forty Thieves Restaurant D. 42nd St. Theaters

45. A. Franco Franceschini B. Amos Franchini 45.___
C. Sandra Franceschia D. Lilie Franchinesca

Questions 46-50.

SPELLING

DIRECTIONS: In each question, one of the words is misspelled. Select the letter of the misspelled word. *PRINT THE LETTER OF THE CORRECT ANSWER IN THE SPACE AT THE RIGHT.*

46. A. option B. extradite 46.___
C. comparitive D. jealousy

47. A. handicaped B. assurance 47.___
C. sympathy D. speech

48. A. recommend B. carraige 48.___
C. disapprove D. independent

49. A. ingenuity B. tenet (opinion) 49.___
C. uncanny D. intrigueing

50. A. arduous B. hideous 50.___
C. fervant D. companies

KEY (CORRECT ANSWERS)

1. A	11. D	21. A	31. B	41. C
2. B	12. B	22. D	32. B	42. D
3. D	13. D	23. C	33. C	43. B
4. B	14. B	24. A	34. D	44. D
5. D	15. A	25. C	35. C	45. C
6. C	16. B	26. D	36. C	46. C
7. A	17. C	27. D	37. B	47. A
8. C	18. D	28. B	38. D	48. B
9. D	19. A	29. A	39. A	49. D
10. B	20. C	30. C	40. A	50. C

EXAMINATION SECTION
TEST 1

DIRECTIONS: Each question or incomplete statement is followed by several suggested answers or completions. Select the one that BEST answers the question or completes the statement. *PRINT THE LETTER OF THE CORRECT ANSWER IN THE SPACE AT THE RIGHT.*

1. Which of the following is the acceptable format for typing the date line? 1.___
   A. 12/2/96
   B. December 2, 1996
   C. December 2nd, 1996
   D. Dec. 2 1996

2. When typing a letter, which of the following is INACCURATE? 2.___
   A. If the letter is to be more than one page long, subsequent sheets should be blank, but should match the letterhead sheet in size, color, weight, and texture.
   B. Long quoted material must be centered and single-spaced internally.
   C. Quotation marks must be used when there is long quoted material.
   D. Double spacing is used above and below tables and long quotations to set them off from the rest of the material.

3. Which of the following is INACCURATE? 3.___
   A. When an addressee's title in an inside address would overrun the center of a page, it's best to carry part of the title over to another line and to indent it by two spaces.
   B. It is permissible to use ordinal numbers in an inside address.
   C. In addresses involving street numbers under three, the number is written out in full.
   D. In the inside address, suite, apartment or room numbers should be placed on the line after the street address.

4. All of the following are common styles of business letters EXCEPT 4.___
   A. simplified
   B. block
   C. direct
   D. executive

5. Please select the two choices below that correctly represent how a continuation sheet heading may be typed. 5.___

I. Page 2
Mr. Alan Post
June 25, 1996

II. Page 2
Mr. Alan Post
6-25-96

III. Mr. Alan Post -2- June 25, 1996

IV. Mr. Alan Post -2- 6-25-96

The CORRECT answer is:
A. I,II B. II,III C. I,III D. II,IV

6. Which of the following is INCORRECT? 6.___
It is
A. permissible to abbreviate honorifics in the inside address
B. permissible to abbreviate company or organizational names, departmental designations, or organizational titles in the inside address
C. permissible to use abbreviations in the inside address if they have been used on the printed letterhead and form part of the official company name
D. sometimes permissible to omit the colon after the salutation

7. Which of the following is INCORRECT? 7.___
A. The subject line of a letter gives the main idea of the message as succinctly as possible.
B. If a letter contains an enclosure, there should be a notation indicating this.
C. Important enclosures ought to be listed numerically and described.
D. An enclosure notation should be typed flush with the right margin.

8. Which of the following is INACCURATE about inside addresses? 8.___
A. An intraoffice or intracompany mail stop number such as DA 3C 61B is put after the organization or company name with at least two spaces intervening.
B. Words such as *Avenue* should not be abbreviated.
C. With the exception of runovers, the inside address should not be more than five full lines.
D. The inside address includes the recipient's courtesy or honorific title and his or her full name on line one; the recipient's title on the next line; the recipient's official organizational affiliation on the next line; the street address on the penultimate line; and the city, state, and zip code on the last line.

9. Which of the following is an INCORRECT example of how to copy recipients when using copy notation? 9.___

A. cc: Martin A. Sheen

B. cc: Ms. Connors
Ms. Grogan
Ms. Reynolds

C. CC: Martin A. Sheen

D. cc: Mr. Right
Mr. Wrong
Mr. Perfect

10. When typing a memo, all of the following are true EXCEPT 10.___
A. it is permissible to use an abbreviation like 1/1/91
B. the subject line should be underlined
C. titles such as *Mr.* or *Dr.* are usually not used on the *To* line
D. unless the memo is very short, paragraphs should be single-spaced and double spacing should be used to separate the paragraphs from each other

11. When typing a letter, which of the following is INACCURATE? 11.___
A. Paragraphs in business letters are usually single-spaced, with double spacing separating them from each other.
B. Margin settings used on subsequent sheets should match those used on the letterhead sheet.
C. If the message contains an enumerated list, it is best to block and center the listed material by five or six more spaces, right and left.
D. A quotation of more than three typed lines must be single-spaced and centered on the page.

12. A letter that is to be signed by Hazel Alice Putney, but written by Mary Jane Roberts, and typed by Alice Carol Bell would CORRECTLY bear the following set of initials: 12.___
A. HAP:MJR:acb
B. HAP:MJR:ab
C. HAP:mjr:acb
D. HAP:mjr:ab

13. Which of the following is INCORRECT? 13.___
A. My dear Dr. Jones:
B. Dear Accounting Department:
C. Dear Dr. Jones:
D. Dear Mr. Al Lee, Esq.:

14. Which of the following is INCORRECT? 14.___
A. Bcc stands for blind copy or blind courtesy copy.
B. When a blind copy is used, the notation bcc appears only on the original.
C. When a blind copy is used, the notation may appear in the top left corner of the letterhead sheet.
D. If following a letter style that uses indented paragraphs, the postscript should be indented in exactly the same manner.

15. All of the following are true of the complimentary close EXCEPT 15.___
A. it is typed two lines beneath the last line of the message
B. when using a minimal punctuation system, you may omit the comma in the complimentary close if you have used a colon in the salutation
C. where the complimentary close is placed may vary
D. the first word of the complimentary close is capitalized

16. When typing a letter, which of the following is INACCURATE? 16.___
    A. Tables should be centered.
    B. If the letter is to be more than one page long, at least three lines of the message itself should be carried over.
    C. The message begins two lines below the salutation in almost all letter styles.
    D. Triple spacing should be used above and below lists to set them off from the rest of the letter.

17. Which one of the following is INCORRECT? 17.___
    A. When used, special mailing instructions should be indicated on both the envelope and the letter itself.
    B. Depending upon the length of the message and the available space, special mailing instructions are usually typed flush left, about four spaces below the date line and about two lines above the first line of the inside address.
    C. Certification, registration, special delivery, and overseas air mail are all considered special mailing instructions.
    D. Special mailing instructions should not be typed in capital letters.

18. Which of the following is INCORRECT? 18.___
    A. When a letter is intended to be personal or confidential, these instructions are typewritten in capital letters on the envelope and on the letter itself.
    B. When a letter is intended to be personal or confidential, these instructions are typewritten in capital letters on the envelope, but not on the letter.
    C. A letter marked PERSONAL is an eyes-only communication for the recipient.
    D. A letter marked CONFIDENTIAL means that the recipient and any other authorized person may open and read it.

19. All of the following are true in regard to copy notation EXCEPT 19.___
    A. when included in a letter, a copy notation should be typed flush with the left margin, two lines below the signature block or two lines below any preceding notation
    B. copy notation should appear after writer/typist initials and/or enclosure notations, if these are used
    C. the copy recipient's full name and address should be indicated
    D. if more than one individual is to be copied, recipients should be listed in alphabetical order according to full name or initials

20. When addressing envelopes, which of the following is INACCURATE? 20.___
   A. When both street address and box number are used, the destination of the letter should be placed on the line just above the city, state, and zip code line.
   B. Special mailing instructions are typed in capital letters below the postage.
   C. Special handling instructions should be typed in capital letters and underlined.
   D. The address should be single-spaced.

21. All of the following should be capitalized EXCEPT the 21.___
   A. first word of a direct quotation
   B. first word in the continuation of a split, single-sentence quotation
   C. names of organizations
   D. names of places and geographic districts, regions, divisions, and locales

22. All of the following are true about capitalization EXCEPT 22.___
   A. words indicating direction and regions are capitalized
   B. the names of rivers, seas, lakes, mountains, and oceans are capitalized
   C. the names of nationalities, tribes, languages, and races are capitalized
   D. civil, military, corporate, royal and noble, honorary, and religious titles are capitalized when they precede a name

23. All of the following are true about capitalization EXCEPT 23.___
   A. key words in the titles of musical, dramatic, artistic, and literary works are capitalized as are the first and last words
   B. the first word of the salutation and of the complimentary close of a letter is capitalized
   C. abbreviations and acronyms are not capitalized
   D. the days of the week, months of the year, holidays, and holy days are capitalized

24. All of the following are true EXCEPT 24.___
   A. an apostrophe indicates the omission of letters in contractions
   B. an apostrophe indicates the possessive case of singular and plural nouns
   C. an apostrophe should not be used to indicate the omission of figures in dates
   D. ellipses are used to indicate the omission of words or sentences within quoted material

25. All of the following are true EXCEPT 25.___
   A. brackets may be used to enclose words or passages in quotations to indicate the insertion of material written by someone other than the original writer
   B. brackets may be used to enclose material that is inserted within material already in parentheses
   C. a dash, rather than a colon, should be used to introduce a list
   D. a colon may be used to introduce a long quotation

26. All of the following are true EXCEPT a(n) 26.___
   A. comma may be used to set off short quotations and sayings
   B. apostrophe is often used to represent the word *per*
   C. dash may be used to indicate a sudden change or break in continuity
   D. dash may be used to set apart an emphatic or defining phrase

27. All of the following are true EXCEPT 27.___
   A. a hyphen may be used as a substitute for the word *to* between figures or words
   B. parentheses are used to enclose material that is not an essential part of the sentence and that, if not included, would not change its meaning
   C. single quotation marks are used to enclose quotations within quotations
   D. semicolons and colons are put inside closing quotation marks

28. All of the following are true EXCEPT 28.___
   A. commas and periods should be put inside closing quotation marks
   B. for dramatic effect, a semicolon may be used instead of a comma to signal longer pauses
   C. a semicolon is used to set off city and state in geographic names
   D. italics are used to represent the titles of magazines and newspapers

29. According to standard rules for typing, two spaces are left after a 29.___
   A. closing parenthesis B. comma
   C. number D. colon

30. All of the following are true EXCEPT 30.___
   A. rounding out large numbers is often acceptable
   B. it is best to use numerical figures to express specific hours, measures, dates, page numbers, coordinates, and addresses
   C. when a sentence begins with a number, it is best to use numerical figures rather than to spell the number out
   D. when two or more numbers appear in one sentence, it is best to spell them out consistently or use numerical figures consistently, regardless of the size of the numbers

31. All of the following are true about word division EXCEPT 31.___
A. words should not be divided on a single letter
B. it is acceptable to carry over two-letter endings
C. the final word in a paragraph should not be divided
D. words in headings should not be divided

32. All of the following are true of word division EXCEPT 32.___
A. it is preferable to divide words of three or more syllables after the consonant
B. it is best to avoid breaking words on more than two consecutive lines
C. words should be divided according to pronunciation
D. two-syllable words are divided at the end of the first syllable

33. All of the following are true of word division EXCEPT 33.___
A. words with short prefixes should be divided after the prefix
B. prefixes and combining forms of more than one syllable should be divided after the first syllable
C. the following word endings are not divided: -gion, -gious, -sial, -sion, -tial, -tion, -tious, -ceous, -cial, -cient, -cion, -cious, and -geous
D. words ending in -er should not be divided if the division could only occur on the -er form

34. All of the following are true about word division EXCEPT 34.___
A. words should be divided so that the part of the word left at the end of the line will suggest the word
B. abbreviations should not be divided
C. the suffixes -able and -ible are usually divided instead of being carried over intact to the next line
D. when the addition of -ed, -est, -er, or a similar ending causes the doubling of a final consonant, the added consonant is carried over

35. All of the following are true of word division EXCEPT 35.___
A. words with doubled consonants are usually divided between those consonants
B. it is permissible to divide contractions
C. words of one syllable should not be split
D. it is best to try to avoid divisions that add a hyphen to an already hyphenated word

36. All of the following are true of word division EXCEPT 36.___
A. dividing proper names should be avoided wherever possible
B. two consonants, preceded and followed by a vowel, are divided after the first consonant
C. even though two adjoining vowels are sounded separately, it is best not to divide between the two vowels
D. it is best not to divide the month and day when typing dates, but the year may be carried over to the next line

37. Which of the following four statements are CORRECT? It would be acceptable to divide the word 37.___
   I. *organization* after the first *a* in the word
   II. *recommend* after the first *m*
   III. *interface* between the *r* and the *f*
   IV. *development* between the *e* and the *l*

   The CORRECT answer is:
   A. I *only* B. II, III
   C. II *only* D. I, II, III

38. Which of the following is divided INCORRECTLY? 38.___
   A. usu-ally B. call-ing
   C. pro-blem D. micro-computer

39. Which of the following is divided INCORRECTLY? 39.___
   A. imag-inary B. commun-ity
   C. manage-able D. commun-ion

40. Which of the following is divided INCORRECTLY? 40.___
   A. spa-ghetti B. retro-spective
   C. proof-reader D. fix-ed

41. Which of the following is divided INCORRECTLY? 41.___
   A. Mr. Han-rahan B. control-lable
   C. pro-jectile D. proj-ect

42. Which of the following is divided INCORRECTLY? 42.___
   A. prom-ise B. han-dling
   C. have-n't D. pro-duce

43. Which of the following is divided INCORRECTLY? 43.___
   A. ship-ped B. audi-ble
   C. hypo-crite D. refer-ring

44. Which of the following is divided INCORRECTLY? 44.___
   A. particu-lar B. spac-ious
   C. chang-ing D. capac-ity

45. There is a critical need to develop the ability to control the mind, especailly the ability to stop repeating negative thoughts. Often, when we must swallow our anger, we are left running an enless tape of thoughts. We can't stop thinking about what the person said and what we should have said in response. To combat this tendency, it is helpful to practice witnessing our thoughts. If we can remain detached from them, we won't fuel them, and they will just run out of gas. As we watch them, we also learn alot about ourselves. The catch here is not to judge them. Judging may lead to selfblaming, blaming others, excuses, rationalizations, and other thoughts that just add fuel. Another technique is is substituting positive thoughts for negative ones. 45.___

It is difficult to do this in the "heat of the moment". With practice, however, its possible to train the mind to do what we want it to do and to contain what we want it to contain. A mind is like a garden -- we can weed it, or we can let it grow wild.
The above paragraph contains a number of typographical errors.
How many lines in this paragraph contain typographical errors?
A. 5 B. 6 C. 8 D. 9

KEY (CORRECT ANSWERS)

1. B	11. D	21. B	31. B	41. A
2. C	12. A	22. A	32. A	42. A
3. D	13. D	23. C	33. B	43. A
4. C	14. B	24. C	34. C	44. B
5. C	15. B	25. C	35. B	45. C
6. B	16. D	26. B	36. C	
7. D	17. D	27. D	37. B	
8. B	18. B	28. C	38. C	
9. D	19. C	29. D	39. B	
10. B	20. C	30. C	40. D	

TEST 2

DIRECTIONS: Each sentence may or may not contain problems in capitalization or punctuation. If there is an error, select the number of the underlined part that must be changed to make the sentence correct. If the sentence has no error, select choice E. No sentence contains more than one error.

1. Is the choice for President (A) of the company (B) George Dawson (C) or Marilyn Kappel? (D) No error (E) — 1.____

2. "To tell you the truth, (A) I was really disappointed (B) that our Fall (C) percentages did not show more sales growth," (D) remarked the bookkeeper. No error (E) — 2.____

3. Bruce gave his Uncle (A) clear directions to go south (B) on Maplewood Drive, (C) turn left at the intersection with Birch Lane, and then proceed for two miles until he reached Columbia County. (D) No error (E) — 3.____

4. Janet hopes to transfer to a college (A) in the east (B) (C) during her junior (D) year. No error (E) — 4.____

5. The Declaration (A) of (B) Independence states (C) that we have the right to the pursuit of Happiness, (D) but it doesn't guarantee that we'll ever find it. No error (E) — 5.____

6. We campaigned hard for the mayor (A), (B) but we're (C) still not sure if he'll win against Senator (D) Frankovich. No error (E) — 6.____

7. Mr. Butler's (A) Ford (B) was parked right behind our's (C) on Atlantic Avenue. (D) No error (E) — 7.____

8. "I respect your opinion, but I cannot agree with it," commented my grandmother. No error 8.____
A B C D E

9. My friends, of course, were surprised when I did so well on the Math section of the test. No error 9.____
A B C D E

10. Dr. Vogel and Senator Rydell decided that the meeting would be held on February 6, in Ithaca, New York. No error 10.____
A B C D E

11. "Frank do you understand what we're telling you?" asked the doctor. No error 11.____
A B C D E

12. When I asked my daughter what she knew about politics she claimed she knew nothing. No error 12.____
A B C D E

13. "If you went to my high school, dad, you'd see things differently," snapped Sean. No error 13.____
A A B C D E

14. In Carlos' third year of high school, he took geometry, psychology, french, and chemistry. No error 14.____
A B B C D E

15. "When you enter the building," the guard instructed us, "turn left down the long, winding corridor." No error 15.____
A B C D E

16. We hope to spend a weekend in the Catskill Mountains in the spring, and we'd like to go to Florida in January. No error 16.____
A B C D E

17. A clerk in the department of Justice asked Carol and me if we were there on business or just sight-seeing. No error 17.____
A B C D E

18. Jamie joined a cult, Harry's in a rock band, and Carol-Ann is studying chinese literature at the University of Southern California. No error 18.___
A: cult, B: 's C: chinese D: University E: No error

19. Parker Flash asked if my band had ever played at the Purple Turnip a club in Orinoco Hills. No error 19.___
A: asked_if B: Purple C: Turnip_a D: Hills E: No error

20. "The gift of the Magi" is a short story by O'Henry that deals with the sad ironies of life. No error 20.___
A: gift B: of C: the D: Magi E: No error

21. Darwin's theory was developed, as a result of his trip to the Galapagos Islands. No error 21.___
A: 's B: theory C: developed, D: Islands E: No error

22. Is 10 Downing street the address of Sherlock Holmes or the British Prime Minister? No error 22.___
A: Downing B: street C: British D: ? E: No error

23. While President Johnson was in Office, his Great Society program passed a great deal of important legislation. No error 23.___
A: President B: Office C: , D: Great D: Society E: No error

24. If, as the American Industrial Health Council's study says, one out of every five cancers today is caused by the workplace it is a tragic indictment of what is happening there. No error 24.___
A: If, B: Council C: 's D: workplace_it E: No error

25. According to the Articles of Confederation, Congress could issue money, but it could not prevent States from issuing their own money. No error 25.___
A: of B: Congress C: money, D: States E: No error

26. "I'd really like to know whos going to be shoveling the driveway this winter," said Laverne. No error 26.___
A: know_whos B: whos C: winter D: ," E: No error

27. According to Carl Jung_ the Swiss psychologist, playing with fantasy is the key to creativity. No error — A (Jung_), B (Swiss), C (psychologist,), D (key), E (No error) 27.___

28. Don't you find it odd that people would prefer jumping off the Golden Gate bridge to jumping off other bridges in the area? No error — A ('t), B (bridge), C (area), D (?), E (No error) 28.___

29. While driving through the South, we saw many of the sites of famous Civil war battles. No error — A (South), B (,), C (war), D (battles), E (No error) 29.___

30. Although I have always valued my Grandmother's china, I prefer her collection of South American art. No error — A (Grandmother), B ('s), C (china), D (South), E (No error) 30.___

KEY (CORRECT ANSWERS)

1. A	11. A	21. C
2. C	12. B	22. B
3. A	13. C	23. B
4. B	14. D	24. D
5. D	15. E	25. D
6. E	16. E	26. B
7. C	17. B	27. A
8. E	18. C	28. B
9. D	19. C	29. C
10. E	20. A	30. A

EXAMINATION SECTION

DIRECTIONS: Each question or incomplete statement is followed by several suggested answers or completions. Select the one that BEST answers the question or completes the statement. *PRINT THE LETTER OF THE CORRECT ANSWER IN THE SPACE AT THE RIGHT.*

Questions 1-15:
For each of the following questions, PRINT on the space at the right the word TRUE if the statement is true, or FALSE if the statement is false.

1. A typist who discovers an obvious grammatical error in a report she is typing should, under ordinary circumstances, copy the material as it was given to her. 1.______

2. The initials of the typist who typed a business letter generally appear on the letter. 2.______

3. It is considered POOR letter form to have *only* the complimentary close and the signature on the second page of a business letter. 3.______

4. Correspondence which is filed according to dates of letters is said to be filed chronologically. 4.______

5. It is *usually* unnecessary to proofread punctuation marks in a report. 5.______

6. The use of window envelopes *reduces* probability of mailing a letter to the wrong address. 6.______

7. Letter size paper is *usually* longer than legal size paper. 7.______

8. It is considered GOOD typing form to have two spaces following a comma. 8.______

9. Both sheets of a two-page typed letter MUST be letterheads. 9.______

10. Before removing a typed letter from the typewriter, the typist should read the copy so that corrections may be made neatly. 10.______

11. When alphabetizing names, you should ALWAYS disregard first names. 11.______

12. When filing a large number of cards according to the name on each card, it is generally a *good* procedure to alphabetize the cards FIRST. 12.______

13. When a report may be filed in a subject file under two headings, it is *good* practice to make a cross reference. 13.______

14. If an essential point has been omitted in a business letter, it is usually considered *good* letter form to include this point in a brief postscript. 14.______

15. Rough draft copies of a report should generally be single-spaced. 15.______

Questions 16-22:
The following items consist of problems in arithmetic. Print in the space at the right the word TRUE if the statement is true, and FALSE if the statement is false.

16. If the rate for first-class mail is 37 cents for each ounce or fraction of an ounce and 23 cents for each ounce or fraction of an ounce above one ounce, then the total cost of sending by first-class mail three letters weighing 1-1/2 ounces, 2 ounces, and 2-1/2 ounces, respectively, would be $1.80. 16.______

17. A typist, who in one hour typed a report consisting of five pages with 60 lines per page and 10 words per line, would have typed at the rate of 45 words per minute. 17.______

18. If a department store employs 45 clerks, 21 typists, and 18 stenographers, the percentage of these employees who are typists is 25%. 18.______

19. If four typists, who type at the same rate of speed, type 1,000 letters in 12 hours, then it will take six typists nine hours to type 1,000 letters. 19.______

20. If 15% of a stenographer's time is spent in taking dictation and 45% of her time is taken up in transcribing her notes, then she has a remainder of two-fifths of her time for performing other duties. 20.______

21. A typist completed 14 pages of a 24-page report before being asked to speak briefly with her employer, then typed the remaining 10 pages. Up until the time she spoke with her employer, the typist had already completed approximately 58% of the report. 21.______

22. Employee A types at a rate of 48 words per minute, while Employee B types at a rate of 54 words per minute. If both employees spend exactly 2-1/4 hours typing reports, Employee B will have typed approximately 810 more words than Employee A. 22.______

Questions 23-54:
Each of the following items consists of two words preceded by the letters A and B. In each item, *one* of the words may be spelled INCORRECTLY, or *both* words may be spelled CORRECTLY. If one of the words is spelled incorrectly, print in the space at the right the letter corresponding to the incorrect word. If both are spelled correctly, print the answer C.

23. A. accessible B. artifical 23.______

24. A. feild B. arranged 24.______

25. A. admittence B. hastily 25.______

26. A. easely B. readily 26.______

27. A. pursue B. decend 27.______

28. A. measure B. laboratory 28.______

29. A. exausted B. traffic 29.______

30. A. discussion B. unpleasant 30.______

31. A. campaign B. murmer 31.______

32. A. guarantee B. sanatary 32.______

33. A. communication B. safty 33.______

34. A. numerus B. celebration 34.______

35. A. nourish B. begining 35.______

36. A. courious B. witness 36.______

37. A. undoubtedly B. thoroughly 37.______

38. A. justified B. offering 38.______

39. A. predjudice B. license 39.______

40. A. label B. pamphlet 40.______

41. A. bulletin B. physical 41.______

42. A. assure B. exceed 42.______

43. A. advantagous B. evident 43.______

44. A. benefit B. occured 44. ______

45. A. acquire B. graditude 45. ______

46. A. amenable B. boundry 46. ______

47. A. deceive B. voluntary 47. ______

48. A. imunity B. conciliate 48. ______

49. A. acknoledge B. presume 49. ______

50. A. substitute B. prespiration 50. ______

51. A. reputible B. announce 51. ______

52. A. luncheon B. wretched 52. ______

53. A. regrettable B. proficiency 53. ______

54. A. rescind B. dissappoint 54. ______

Questions 55-72:
Each of the sentences that follow may be classified MOST appropriately under one of the following three categories:

A. *faulty* because of incorrect grammar
B. *faulty* because of incorrect punctuation
C. *correct*

Examine each sentence, then select the best answer as listed above and place the letter in the space at the right. All incorrect sentences contain only ONE type of error. Consider a sentence correct if it contains none of the types of errors mentioned, even though there may be other correct ways of expressing the same thought.

55. He sent the notice to the clerk who hired you yesterday. 55. ______

56. It must be admitted, however that you were not informed of this change. 56. ______

57. Only the employees who have served in this grade for at least two years are eligible for promotion. 57. ______

58. The work was divided equally between she and Mary. 58. ______

59. He thought that you were not available at the time. 59. ______

60. When the messenger returns; please give him this package. 60. ______

61. The new secretary prepared, typed, addressed, and delivered, the notices. 61. ______

62. Walking into the room, his desk can be seen at the rear. 62. ______

63. Although John has worked here longer then she, he produces a smaller amount of work. 63. ______

64. She said she could of typed this report yesterday. 64. ______

65. Neither one of these procedures are adequate for the efficient performance of this task. 65. ______

66. The typewriter is the tool of the typist; the cash register, the tool of the cashier. 66. ______

67. "The assignment must be completed as soon as possible" said the supervisor. 67. ______

68. As you know, office handbooks are issued to all new employees. 68. ______

69. Writing a speech is sometimes easier than to deliver it before an audience. 69. ______

70. Mr. Brown our accountant, will audit the accounts next week. 70. ______

71. Give the assignment to whomever is able to do it most efficiently. 71. ______

72. The supervisor expected either your or I to file these reports. 72. ______

Questions 73-90:
For each of the following test items, print the letter in the space at the right of the answer that BEST completes the statement.

73. A PREVALENT practice is one which is 73. ______
A. rare B. unfair C. widespread D. correct

74. To prepare a RECAPITULATION means *most nearly* to prepare a 74. ______
A. summary B. revision C. defense D. decision

75. An ADVERSE decision is one which is 75. ______
A. unfavorable B. unwise
C. anticipated D. backwards

76. A COMMENDATORY report is one which 76. ______
A. expresses praise B. contains contradictions
C. is too detailed D. is threatening

77. "The council will DEFER action on this matter." The word DEFER means *most nearly* 77. ______

A. hasten B. consider C. postpone D. reject

78. MEAGER results are those which are 78. ______

A. satisfactory
B. scant
C. unexpected
D. praiseworthy

79. An ARDUOUS job assignment 79. ______

A. requires much supervision
B. is laborious
C. absorbs one's interest
D. is lengthy

80. "This employee was IMPLICATED." The word IMPLICATED *most nearly* means 80. ______

A. demoted B. condemned C. involved D. accused

81. To be DETAINED means *most nearly* to be 81. ______

A. entertained
B. held back
C. sent away
D. scolded

82. An AMIABLE person is one who is 82. ______

A. active B. pleasing C. thrifty D. foolish

83. A UNIQUE procedure is one which is 83. ______

A. simple B. uncommon C. useless D. ridiculous

84. The word REPLENISH means *most nearly* to 84. ______

A. give up B. punish C. refill D. empty

85. A CONCISE report is one which is 85. ______

A. logical B. favorable C. brief D. intelligent

86. ELATED means *most nearly* 86. ______

A. lengthened B. matured C. excited D. youthful

87. SANCTION means *most nearly* 87. ______

A. approval B. delay C. priority D. veto

88. EGOTISTIC means *most nearly* 88. ______

A. tiresome
B. self-centered
C. sly
D. smartly attired

89. TRITE means *most nearly* 89. ______

A. brilliant
B. unusual
C. funny
D. commonplace

90. FESTIVE means *most nearly* 90. ______

A. edible B. joyous C. proud D. serene

KEY (CORRECT ANSWERS)

1. F	31. B	61. B
2. T	32. B	62. A
3. T	33. B	63. C
4. T	34. A	64. A
5. F	35. B	65. A
6. T	36. A	66. C
7. F	37. C	67. B
8. F	38. C	68. C
9. F	39. A	69. A
10. T	40. C	70. B
11. F	41. C	71. A
12. T	42. C	72. A
13. T	43. A	73. C
14. F	44. B	74. A
15. F	45. B	75. A
16. F	46. B	76. A
17. F	47. C	77. C
18. T	48. A	78. B
19. F	49. A	79. B
20. T	50. B	80. C
21. T	51. A	81. B
22. T	52. C	82. B
23. B	53. C	83. B
24. A	54. B	84. C
25. A	55. A	85. C
26. A	56. B	86. C
27. B	57. C	87. A
28. C	58. A	88. B
29. A	59. C	89. D
30. C	60. B	90. B

EXAMINATION SECTION

DIRECTIONS: Each question or incomplete statement is followed by several suggested answers or completions. Select the one that BEST answers the question or completes the statement. *PRINT THE LETTER OF THE CORRECT ANSWER IN THE SPACE AT THE RIGHT.*

Questions 1-25

Each sentence in questions 1-25 includes four words with letters over them. One of these words has been typed incorrectly. Indicate the misspelled word by printing the letter in the space at the right.

A B
1. If the administrator attempts to withold information, 1.____
C
there is a good likelihood that there will be serious
D
repercussions.

A B C
2. He condescended to apologize, but we felt that a beligerent 2.____
D
person should not occupy an influential position.

A B C
3. Despite the sporadic delinquent payments of his indebted- 3.____
D
ness, Mr. Johnson has been an exemplery customer.

A B
4. He was appreciative of the support he consistantly 4.____
C D
acquired, but he felt that he had waited an inordinate
length of time for it.

A B
5. Undeniably they benefited from the establishment of a 5.____
C D
receivership, but the question or statutary limitations
remained unresolved.

A
6. Mr. Smith profered his hand as an indication that he 6.____
B C
considered it a viable contract, but Mr. Nelson alluded
D
to the fact that his colleagues had not been consulted.

A B
7. The treatments were beneficial according to the optomo- 7.____
C D
trists, and the consensus was that minimal improvement
could be expected.

A
8. Her frivalous manner was unbecoming because the air of 8.____
B C D
solemnity at the cemetery was pervasive.

A
9. The clandestine meetings were designed to make the two 9.____
B C
adversaries more amicible, but they served only to
D
intensify their emnity.

A
10. Do you think that his innovative ideas and financial 10.____
B C D
acumen will help stabalize the fluctuations of the stock
market?

A
11. In order to keep a perpetual inventory, you will have to 11.____
B C D
keep an uninterrupted surveillance of all the miscellaneous
stock.

A
12. She used the art of pursuasion on the children because 12.____
B C D
she found that caustic remarks had no perceptible effect
on their behavior.

A B
13. His sacreligious outbursts offended his constituents, and 13.____
C D
he was summarily removed from office by the City Council.

A B
14. They exhorted the contestants to greater efforts, but the 14.____
C
exhorbitant costs in terms of energy expended resulted in
D
a feeling of lethargy.

A B
15. Since he was knowledgable about illicit drugs, he was 15.____
C D
served with a subpoena to appear for the prosecution.

A B
16. In spite of his lucid statements, they denigrated his 16.____
C D
report and decided it should be succintly paraphrased.

A B
17. The discussion was not germane to the contraversy, but 17.____
C D
the indicted man's insistence on further talk was allowed.

A B
18. The legislators were enervated by the distances they had 18.____
C D
traveled during the election year to fulfil their speaking
engagements.

A B C
19. The plaintiffs' attornies charged the defendant in the 19.____
D
case with felonious assault.

A B
20. It is symptomatic of the times that we try to placate 20.____
C
all, but a proposal for new forms of disciplinery action
D
was promulgated by the staff.

A
21. A worrysome situation has developed as a result of the 21.____
B C
assessment that absenteeism is increasing despite our
D
conscientious efforts.

A B
22. I concurred with the credit manager that it was practi- 22.____
C
cable to charge purchases on a biennial basis, and the
D
company agreed to adhear to this policy.

A B C
23. The pastor was chagrined and embarassed by the irreverent 23.____
D
conduct of one of his parishioners.

A B C
24. His inate seriousness was belied by his flippant 24.____
D
demeanor.

A B C
25. It was exceedingly regrettable that the excessive number 25.____
D
of challanges in the court delayed the start of the
trial.

Questions 26-45.

In each of the following sentences, numbered 26-45, there may be an error. Indicate the appropriate correction by printing the corresponding letter in the space at the right. If the sentence is correct as is, indicate this by printing the corresponding letter in the space at the right. Unnecessary changes will be considered incorrect.

26. In that building there seemed to be representatives of Teachers College, the Veterans Bureau, and the Businessmen's Association. 26.____
A. Teacher's College
B. Veteran's Bureau
C. Businessmens Association
D. correct as is

27. In his travels, he visited St. Paul, San Francisco, Springfield, Ohio, and Washington, D.C.. 27.____
A. Ohio and
B. Saint Paul
C. Washington, D.C.
D. correct as is

28. As a result of their purchasing a controlling interest in the syndicate, it was well-known that the Bureau of Labor Statistics' calculations would be unimportant. 28.____
A. of them purchasing
B. well known
C. Statistics
D. correct as is

29. Walter Scott, Jr.'s, attempt to emulate his father's success was doomed to failure. 29.____
A. Junior's,
B. Scott's, Jr.,
C. Scott, Jr.'s attempt
D. correct as is

30. About B.C. 250 the Romans invaded Great Britain, and remains of their highly developed civilization can still be seen. 30.____
A. 250 B.C.
B. Britain and
C. highly-developed
D. correct as is

31. The two boss's sons visited the children's department. 31.____
A. bosses
B. bosses'
C. childrens'
D. correct as is

32. Miss Amex not only approved the report, but also decided that it needed no revision. 32.____
A. report; but
B. report but
C. report. But
D. correct as is

33. Here's brain food in a jiffy--economical too! 33.____
A. economical too!
B. 'brain food'
C. jiffy-economical
D. correct as is

34. She said, "He likes the "Gatsby Look" very much." 34.____
A. said "He
B. "he
C. 'Gatsby Look'
D. correct as is

35. We anticipate that we will be able to visit them briefly in Los Angeles on Wednes-
day after a 5-day visit. 35.____
A. Wednes-
B. 5-day
C. briefly
D. correct as is

36. She passed all her tests, and, she now has a good position. 36.____
A. tests, and she
B. past
C. tests;
D. correct as is

37. The billing clerk said, "I will send the bill today"; however, that was a week ago, and it hasn't arrived yet! 37.____
A. today;"
B. today,"
C. ago and
D. correct as is

38. "She types at more-than-average speed," Miss Smith said, "but I feel that it is a result of marvelous concentration and self control on her part." 38.____
   A. more than average
   B. "But
   C. self-control
   D. correct as is

39. The state of Alaska, the largest state in the union, is also the northernmost state. 39.____
   A. Union
   B. Northernmost State
   C. State of Alaska
   D. correct as is

40. The memoirs of Ex-President Nixon, will sell more copies than Six Crises, the book he wrote in the 60's. 40.____
   A. Six Crises
   B. ex-President
   C. 60s
   D. correct as is

41. He spoke on his favorite topic, "Why We Will Win." (How could I stop him?) 41.____
   A. Win".
   B. him?).
   C. him)?
   D. correct as is

42. "All any insurance policy is, is a contract for services," said my insurance agent, Mr. Newton. 42.____
   A. Insurance Policy
   B. Insurance Agent
   C. policy is is a
   D. correct as is

43. Inasmuch as the price list has not been up dated, we should send it to the printer. 43.____
   A. In as much
   B. updated
   C. pricelist
   D. correct as is

44. We feel that "Our know-how" is responsible for the improvement in technical developments. 44.____
   A. "our
   B. know how
   C. that,
   D. correct as is

45. Did Cortez conquer the Incas? the Aztecs? the South American Indians? 45.____
   A. Incas, the Aztecs, the South American Indians?
   B. Incas; the Aztecs; the South American Indians?
   C. south American Indians?
   D. correct as is

Questions 46-70.
In the article which follows, certain words or groups of words are underlined and numbered. The underlined word or group of words may be incorrect because they present an error in grammer, usage, sentence structure, capitalization, diction, or punctuation. For each numbered word or group of words, there is an identically numbered question consisting of four choices based only on the underlined portion. For each question numbered 46-70, indicate the best choice by printing the corresponding letter in the space at the right. Unnecessary changes will be considered incorrect.

TIGERS VIE FOR CITY CHAMPIONSHIP

In their second year of varsity football, the North Side Tigers have gained a shot at the city championship. Last Saturday in the play-offs, the Tigers defeated the Western High School Cowboys[46], thus eliminated that team from contention. Most of the credit for the team's improvement must go to Joe Harris, the coach. [47] To play as well as they do now, the coach must have given the team superior instruction. There is no doubt that, [48] if a coach is effective, his influence is over many young minds.

With this major victory behind them, the Tigers can now look forward [49] to meet the defending champions, the Revere Minutemen, in the finals.

The win over the Cowboys was [50] due to North Side's supremacy in the air. The Tigers' players have the advantage of strength and of [51] being speedy. Our sterling quarterback, Butch Carter, a master of the long pass, used [52] these kind of passes to bedevil the boys from Western. As a matter of fact, if the Tigers [53] would have used the passing offense earlier in the game, the score would have been more one sided. Butch, by the way, our all-around senior student, has already been tapped for bigger things. Having the highest marks in his class, [54] Barton College has offered him a scholarship.

The team's defense is another story. During the last few weeks, neither the linebackers nor the safety man [55] have shown sufficient ability to contain their opponents' running game. In the city final, [56] the defensive unit's failing to complete it's assignments may lead to disaster. However, the coach said that this unit [57] not only has been cooperative, but also the coach praised their eagerness to learn. He also said that this team [58] has not and never will give up. This kind of spirit is contagious[59], therefore I predict that the Tigers will win because I have [60] affection and full confidence in the team.

One of the happy surprises this season is Peter Yisko, our punter. Peter [61] is in the United States for only two years. When he was in grammar school in the old country, it was not necessary for him [62] to have studied hard. Now, he depends on the football team to help him with his English. Everybody [63] but the team mascot and I have been pressed into service. Peter was ineligible last year when he [64] learned that he would only obtain half of the credits he had completed in Europe. Nevertheless, he attended occasional practice sessions, but he soon found out that, if one wants to be a successful player, [65] you must realize that regular practice is required. In fact, if a team is to be successful, it is necessary that everyone [66] be present for all practice sessions. "The life of a football player," says Peter, "is better than [67] a scholar."

Facing the Minutemen, the Tigers will meet their most formidable opposition yet. This team [68] is not only gaining a bad reputation but also indulging in illegal practices on the field. They [69] can't hardly object to us being technical about penalties under these circumstances. As far as the Minutemen are concerned, a [70] victory will taste sweet like a victory should.

46. A. , that eliminated that team
    B. and they were eliminated
    C. and eliminated them
    D. correct as is

46.____

47. A. To make them play as well as they do 47.____
B. Having played so well
C. After they played so well
D. correct as is

48. A. if coaches are effective; they have influence over 48.____
B. to be effective, a coach influences
C. if a coach is effective, he influences
D. correct as is

49. A. to meet with B. to meeting 49.____
C. to a meeting of D. correct as is

50. A. because of B. on account of 50.____
C. motivated by D. correct as is

51. A. operating swiftly B. speed 51.____
C. running speedily D. correct as is

52. A. these kinds of pass B. this kind of passes 52.____
C. this kind of pass D. correct as is

53. A. would be used B. had used 53.____
C. were using D. correct as is

54. A. he was offered a scholarship by Barton College. 54.____
B. Barton College offered a scholarship to him.
C. a scholarship was offered him by Barton College.
D. correct as is

55. A. had shown B. were showing 55.____
C. has shown D. correct as is

56. A. the defensive unit failing to complete its assignment 56.____
B. the defensive unit's failing to complete its assignment
C. the defensive unit failing to complete it's assignment
D. correct as is

57. A. has been not only cooperative, but also eager to learn 57.____
B. has not only been cooperative, but also shows eagerness to learn
C. has been not only cooperative, but also they were eager to learn
D. correct as is

58. A. has not given up and never will 58.____
B. has not and never would give up
C. has not given up and never will give up
D. correct as is

59. A. . Therefore B. : therefore 59.____
C. --therefore D. correct as is

60. A. full confidence and affection for 60.____
B. affection for and full confidence in
C. affection and full confidence concerning
D. correct as is

61. A. is living B. was living 61.____
C. has been D. correct as is

62. A. to study B. to be studying 62.____
C. to have been studying D. correct as is

63. A. but the team mascot and me has 63.____
B. but the team mascot and myself has
C. but the team mascot and me have
D. correct as is

64. A. only learned that he would obtain half 64.____
B. learned that he would obtain only half
C. learned that he only would obtain half
D. correct as is

65. A. a person B. everyone 65.____
C. one D. correct as is

66. A. is B. will be 66.____
C. shall be D. correct as is

67. A. to be a scholar B. being a scholar 67.____
C. that of a scholar D. correct as is

68. A. not only is gaining a bad reputation 68.____
B. is gaining not only a bad reputation
C. is not gaining only a bad reputation
D. correct as is

69. A. can hardly object to us being 69.____
B. can hardly object to our being
C. can't hardly object to our being
D. correct as is

70. A. victory will taste sweet like it should. 70.____
B. victory will taste sweetly as it should taste.
C. victory will taste sweet as a victory should.
D. correct as is

KEY (CORRECT ANSWERS)

1. B	21. A	41. D	61. C
2. C	22. D	42. D	62. A
3. D	23. B	43. B	63. A
4. B	24. A	44. A	64. B
5. D	25. D	45. D	65. C
6. A	26. D	46. C	66. D
7. B	27. C	47. A	67. C
8. A	28. B	48. C	68. D
9. C	29. D	49. B	69. A
10. C	30. A	50. A	70. C
11. D	31. B	51. B	
12. A	32. B	52. C	
13. A	33. D	53. B	
14. C	34. C	54. D	
15. A	35. B	55. C	
16. C	36. A	56. B	
17. B	37. D	57. A	
18. D	38. D	58. B	
19. B	39. A	59. A	
20. C	40. B	60. B	

EXAMINATION SECTION
TEST 1

DIRECTIONS: Each question or incomplete statement is followed by several suggested answers or completions. Select the one that BEST answers the question or completes the statement. *PRINT THE LETTER OF THE CORRECT ANSWER IN THE SPACE AT THE RIGHT.*

1. In order to avoid clogging the works of a typewriter while making an erasure on a page being typed, it is BEST to 1.___
   A. remove the page from the typewriter and then erase
   B. move the carriage to the extreme right or left before you erase
   C. move the paper up until you reach the bottom of the page before you erase
   D. backspace five spaces past the error and then erase

2. In order to make the BEST use of the tabulator when typing many letters, you should set the tabulator to stop at 2.___
   A. right margin and paragraph indentation
   B. right margin and signature line
   C. center of the page and date line
   D. complimentary close and paragraph indentation

3. Suppose your supervisor is on the telephone in his office and an applicant arrives for a scheduled interview with him. 3.___
   Of the following, the BEST procedure to follow ordinarily is to
   A. informally chat with the applicant in your office until your supervisor has finished his phone conversation
   B. escort him directly into your supervisor's office and have him wait for him there
   C. inform your supervisor of the applicant's arrival and try to make the applicant feel comfortable while waiting
   D. have him hang up his coat and tell him to go directly in to see your supervisor

Questions 4-9.

DIRECTIONS: Questions 4 through 9 each consist of a sentence which may or may not be an example of good English usage. Consider grammar, punctuation, spelling, capitalization, awkwardness, etc. Examine each sentence, and then choose the correct statement about it from the four choices below it. If the English usage in the sentence given is better than any of the changes suggested in options B, C, or D, choose option A. Do not choose an option that will change the meaning of the sentence.

4. The report, along with the accompanying documents, were submitted for review. 4.___
   A. This is an example of acceptable writing.
   B. The words *were submitted* should be changed to *was submitted*.
   C. The word *accompanying* should be spelled *accompaning*.
   D. The comma after the word *report* should be taken out.

5. If others must use your files, be certain that they understand how the system works, but insist that you do all the filing and refiling. 5.___
   A. This is an example of acceptable writing.
   B. There should be a period after the word *works*, and the word *but* should start a new sentence.
   C. The words *filing* and *refiling* should be spelled *fileing* and *refileing*.
   D. There should be a comma after the word *but*.

6. The appeal was not considered because of its late arrival. 6.___
   A. This is an example of acceptable writing.
   B. The word *its* should be changed to *it's*.
   C. The word *its* should be changed to *the*.
   D. The words *late arrival* should be changed to *arrival late*.

7. The letter must be read carefuly to determine under which subject it should be filed. 7.___
   A. This is an example of acceptable writing.
   B. The word *under* should be changed to *at*.
   C. The word *determine* should be spelled *determin*.
   D. The word *carefuly* should be spelled *carefully*.

8. He showed potential as an office manager, but he lacked skill in delegating work. 8.___
   A. This is an example of acceptable writing.
   B. The word *delegating* should be spelled *delagating*.
   C. The word *potential* should be spelled *potencial*.
   D. The words *he lacked* should be changed to *was lacking*.

9. His supervisor told him that it would be all right to receive personal mail at the office. 9.___
   A. This is an example of acceptable writing.
   B. The words *all right* should be changed to *alright*.
   C. The word *personal* should be spelled *personel*.
   D. The word *mail* should be changed to *letters*.

Questions 10-13.

DIRECTIONS: Questions 10 through 13 are to be answered SOLELY on the basis of the information given in the following passage.

Typed pages can reflect the simplicity of modern art in a machine age. Lightness and evenness can be achieved by proper layout and balance of typed lines and white space. Instead of solid, cramped masses of uneven, crowded typing, there should be a pleasing balance up and down as well as horizontal.

To have real balance, your page must have a center. The eyes see the center of the sheet slightly above the real center. This is the way both you and the reader see it. Try imagining a line down the center of the page that divides the paper in equal halves. On either side of your paper, white space and blocks of typing need to be similar in size and shape. Although left and right margins should be equal, top and bottom margins need not be as exact. It looks better to hold a bottom border wider than a top margin, so that your typing rests upon a cushion of white space. To add interest to the appearance of the page, try making one paragraph between one-half and two-thirds the size of an adjacent paragraph.

Thus, by taking full advantage of your typewriter, the pages that you type will not only be accurate but will also be attractive.

10. It can be inferred from the passage that the BASIC importance of proper balancing on a typed page is that proper balancing 10.___
    A. makes a typed page a work of modern art
    B. provides exercise in proper positioning of a typewriter
    C. increases the amount of typed copy on the paper
    D. draws greater attention and interest to the page

11. A reader will tend to see the center of a typed page 11.___
    A. somewhat higher than the true center
    B. somewhat lower than the true center
    C. on either side of the true center
    D. about two-thirds of an inch above the true center

12. Which of the following suggestions is NOT given by the passage? 12.___
    A. Bottom margins may be wider than top borders.
    B. Keep all paragraphs approximately the same size.
    C. Divide your page with an imaginary line down the middle.
    D. Side margins should be equalized.

13. Of the following, the BEST title for this passage is: 13.___
    A. INCREASING THE ACCURACY OF THE TYPED PAGE
    B. DETERMINATION OF MARGINS FOR TYPED COPY
    C. LAYOUT AND BALANCE OF THE TYPED PAGE
    D. HOW TO TAKE FULL ADVANTAGE OF THE TYPEWRITER

14. In order to type addresses on a large number of envelopes MOST efficiently, you should 14.___
   A. insert another envelope into the typewriter before removing each typed envelope
   B. take each typed envelope out of the machine before starting the next envelope
   C. insert several envelopes into the machine at one time, keeping all top and bottom edges even
   D. insert several envelopes into the machine at one time, keeping the top edge of each envelope two inches below the top edge of the one beneath it

15. A senior typist has completed copying a statistical report from a rough draft. 15.___
Of the following, the BEST way to be sure that her typing is correct is for the typist to
   A. fold the rough draft, line it up with the typed copy, compare one-half of the columns with the original, and have a co-worker compare the other half
   B. check each line of the report as it is typed and then have a co-worker check each line again after the entire report is finished
   C. have a co-worker add each column and check the totals on the typed copy with the totals on the original
   D. have a co-worker read aloud from the rough draft while the typist checks the typed copy and then have the typist read while the co-worker checks

16. In order to center a heading when typing a report, you should 16.___
   A. measure your typing paper with a ruler and begin the heading one-third of the way in from the left margin
   B. begin the heading at the point on the typewriter scale which is 50 minus the number of letters in the heading
   C. multiply the number of characters in the heading by two and begin the heading that number of spaces in from the left margin
   D. begin the heading at the point on the scale which is equal to the center point of your paper minus one-half the number of characters and spaces in the heading

17. Which of the following recommendations concerning the use of copy paper for making typewritten copies should NOT be followed? 17.___
   A. Copy papers should be checked for wrinkles before being used.
   B. Legal-size copy paper may be folded if it is too large to fit into a convenient drawer space.
   C. When several sheets of paper and carbon paper are being used, they should be fastened with a paper clip at the top after insertion in the typewriter.
   D. For making many carbon copies, thin carbon paper and onionskin should be used.

18. Assume that a new typist, Norma Garcia, has been assigned to work under your supervision and is reporting to work for the first time. You formally introduce Norma to her co-workers and suggest that a few of the other typists explain the office procedures and typing formats to her. The practice of instructing Norma in her duties in this manner is 18.___
   A. *good* because she will be made to feel at home
   B. *good* because she will learn more about routine office tasks from co-workers than from you
   C. *poor* because her co-workers will resent the extra work
   D. *poor* because you will not have enough control over her training

19. Suppose that Jean Brown, a typist, is typing a letter following the same format that she has always used. However, she notices that the other two typists in her office are also typing letters, but are using a different format. Jean is concerned that she might not have been informed of a change in format. 19.___
   Of the following, the FIRST action that Jean should take is to
   A. seek advice from her supervisor as to which format to use
   B. ask the other typists whether she should use a new format for typing letters
   C. disregard the format that the other typists are using and continue to type in the format she had been using
   D. use the format that the other typists are using, assuming that it is a newly accepted method

20. Suppose that the new office to which you have been assigned has put up Christmas decorations, and a Christmas party is being planned by the city agency in which you work. However, nothing has been said about Christmas gifts. 20.___
   It would be CORRECT for you to assume that
   A. you are expected to give a gift to your supervisor
   B. your supervisor will give you a gift
   C. you are expected to give gifts only to your subordinates
   D. you will neither receive gifts nor will you be expected to give any

KEY (CORRECT ANSWERS)

1. B	6. A	11. A	16. D
2. D	7. D	12. B	17. B
3. C	8. A	13. C	18. D
4. B	9. A	14. A	19. A
5. A	10. D	15. D	20. D

TEST 2

DIRECTIONS: Each question or incomplete statement is followed by several suggested answers or completions. Select the one that BEST answers the question or completes the statement. *PRINT THE LETTER OF THE CORRECT ANSWER IN THE SPACE AT THE RIGHT.*

1. The supervisor you assist is under great pressure to meet certain target dates. He has scheduled an emergency meeting to take place in a few days, and he asks you to send out notices immediately. As you begin to prepare the notices, however, you realize he has scheduled the meeting for a Saturday, which is not a working day. Also, you sense that your supervisor is not in a good mood. Which of the following is the MOST effective method of handling this situation? 1.___
   A. Change the meeting date to the first working day after that Saturday and send out the notices.
   B. Change the meeting date to a working day on which his calendar is clear and send out the notices.
   C. Point out to your supervisor that the date is a Saturday.
   D. Send out the notices as they are since you have received specific instructions.

Questions 2-7.

DIRECTIONS: Questions 2 through 7 each consist of a sentence which may or may not be an example of good English usage. Consider grammar, punctuation, spelling, capitalization, awkwardness, etc. Examine each sentence, and then choose the correct statement about it from the four choices below it. If the English usage in the sentence given is better than any of the changes suggested in options B, C, or D, choose option A. Do not choose an option that will change the meaning of the sentence.

2. The typist used an extention cord in order to connect her typewriter to the outlet nearest to her desk. 2.___
   A. This is an example of acceptable writing.
   B. A period should be placed after the word *cord*, and the word *in* should have a capital *I*.
   C. A comma should be placed after the word *typewriter*.
   D. The word *extention* should be spelled *extension*.

3. He would have went to the conference if he had received an invitation. 3.___
   A. This is an example of acceptable writing.
   B. The word *went* should be replaced by the word *gone*.
   C. The word *had* should be replaced by *would have*.
   D. The word *conference* should be spelled *conferance*.

4. In order to make the report neater, he spent many hours rewriting it. 4.____
   A. This is an example of acceptable writing.
   B. The word *more* should be inserted before the word *neater*.
   C. There should be a colon after the word *neater*.
   D. The word *spent* should be changed to *have spent*.

5. His supervisor told him that he should of read the memorandum more carefully. 5.____
   A. This is an example of acceptable writing.
   B. The word *memorandum* should be spelled *memorandom*.
   C. The word *of* should be replaced by the word *have*.
   D. The word *carefully* should be replaced by the word *careful*.

6. It was decided that two separate reports should be written. 6.____
   A. This is an example of acceptable writing.
   B. A comma should be inserted after the word *decided*.
   C. The word *be* should be replaced by the word *been*.
   D. A colon should be inserted after the word *that*.

7. She don't seem to understand that the work must be done as soon as possible. 7.____
   A. This is an example of acceptable writing.
   B. The word *doesn't* should replace the word *don't*.
   C. The word *why* should replace the word *that*.
   D. The word *as* before the word *soon* should be eliminated.

Questions 8-11.

DIRECTIONS: Questions 8 through 11 are to be answered SOLELY on the basis of the following passage.

There is nothing that will take the place of good sense on the part of the stenographer. You may be perfect in transcribing exactly what the dictator says and your speed may be adequate; but without an understanding of the dictator's intent as well as his words, you are likely to be a mediocre secretary.

A serious error that is made when taking dictation is putting down something that does not make sense. Most people who dictate material would rather be asked to repeat and explain than to receive transcribed material which has errors due to inattention or doubt. Many dictators request that their grammar be corrected by their secretaries; but unless specifically asked to do so, secretaries should not do it without first checking with the dictator. Secretaries should be aware that, in some cases, dictators may use incorrect grammar or slang expressions to create a particular effect.

Some people dictate commas, periods, and paragraphs, while others expect the stenographer to know when, where, and how to punctuate. A well-trained secretary should be able to indicate the proper punctuation by listening to the pauses and tones of the dictator's voice.

A stenographer who has taken dictation from the same person for a period of time should be able to understand him under most conditions. By increasing her tact, alertness, and efficiency, a secretary can become more competent.

8. According to the passage, which of the following statements concerning the dictation of punctuation is CORRECT? 8.___
A
   A. dictator may use incorrect punctuation to create a desired style
   B. dictator should indicate all punctuation
   C. stenographer should know how to punctuate based on the pauses and tones of the dictator
   D. stenographer should not type any punctuation if it has not been dictated to her

9. According to the passage, how should secretaries handle grammatical errors in a dictation? 9.___
Secretaries should
   A. *not correct* grammatical errors unless the dictator is aware that this is being done
   B. *correct* grammatical errors by having the dictator repeat the line with proper pauses
   C. *correct* grammatical errors if they have checked the correctness in a grammar book
   D. *correct* grammatical errors based on their own good sense

10. If a stenographer is confused about the method of spacing and indenting of a report which has just been dictated to her, she GENERALLY should 10.___
   A. do the best she can
   B. ask the dictator to explain what she should do
   C. try to improve her ability to understand dictated material
   D. accept the fact that her stenographic ability is not adequate

11. In the last line of the first paragraph, the word *mediocre* means MOST NEARLY 11.___
   A. superior
   B. disregarded
   C. respected
   D. second-rate

12. Assume that is is your responsibility to schedule meetings for your supervisor, who believes in starting these meetings strictly on time. He has told you to schedule separate meetings with Mr. Smith and Ms. Jones, which will last approximately 20 minutes each. You have told Mr. Smith to arrive at 10:00 A.M. and Ms. Jones at 10:30 A.M. Your supervisor will have an hour of free time at 11:00 A.M. At 10:25 A.M., Mr. Smith arrives and states that there was a train delay, and he is sorry that he is late. Ms. Jones has not yet arrived. You do not know who Mr. Smith and Ms. Jones are or what the meetings will be about. 12.___

Of the following, the BEST course of action for you to take is to
A. send Mr. Smith in to see your supervisor; and when Ms. Jones arrives, tell her that your supervisor's first meeting will take more time than he expected
B. tell Mr. Smith that your supervisor has a meeting at 10:30 A.M. and that you will have to reschedule his meeting for another day
C. check with your supervisor to find out if he would prefer to see Mr. Smith immediately or at 11:00 A.M.
D. encourage your supervisor to meet with Mr. Smith immediately because Mr. Smith's late arrival was not intentional

13. Assume that you have been told by your boss not to let anyone disturb him for the rest of the afternoon unless absolutely necessary since he has to complete some urgent work. His supervisor, who is the bureau chief, telephones and asks to speak to him. 13.___
The BEST course of action for you to take is to
A. ask the bureau chief if he can leave a message
B. ask your boss if he can take the call
C. tell the bureau chief that your boss is out
D. tell your boss that his instructions will get you into trouble

14. Which one of the following is the MOST advisable procedure for a stenographer to follow when a dictator asks her to make extra copies of dictated material? 14.___
A. Note the number of copies required at the beginning of the notes.
B. Note the number of copies required at the end of the notes.
C. Make a mental note of the number of copies required to be made.
D. Make a checkmark beside the notes to serve as a reminder that extra copies are required.

15. Suppose that, as you are taking shorthand notes, the dictator tells you that the sentence he has just dictated is to be deleted. 15.___
Of the following, the BEST thing for you to do is to
A. place the correction in the left-hand margin next to the deleted sentence
B. write the word *delete* over the sentence and place the correction on a separate page for corrections
C. erase the sentence and use that available space for the correction
D. draw a line through the sentence and begin the correction on the next available line

16. Assume that your supervisor, who normally dictates at a relatively slow rate, begins dictating to you very rapidly. You find it very difficult to keep up at this speed. Which one of the following is the BEST action to take in this situation? 16.___
    A. Ask your supervisor to dictate more slowly since you are having difficulty.
    B. Continue to take the dictation at the fast speed and fill in the blanks later.
    C. Interrupt your supervisor with a question about the dictation, hoping that when she begins again it will be slower.
    D. Refuse to take the dictation unless given at the speed indicated in your job description.

17. Assume that you have been asked to put a heading on the second, third, and fourth pages of a four-page letter to make sure they can be identified in case they are separated from the first page. 17.___
    Which of the following is it LEAST important to include in such a heading?
    A. Date of the letter
    B. Initials of the typist
    C. Name of the person to whom the letter is addressed
    D. Number of the page

18. Which one of the following is NOT generally accepted when dividing words at the end of a line? 18.___
    Dividing
    A. a hyphenated word at the hyphen
    B. a word immediately after the prefix
    C. a word immediately before the suffix
    D. proper names between syllables

19. In the preparation of a business letter which has two enclosures, the MOST generally accepted of the following procedures to follow is to type 19.___
    A. *See Attached Items* one line below the last line of the body of the letter
    B. *See Attached Enclosures* to the left of the signature
    C. *Enclosures 2* at the left margin below the signature line
    D. nothing on the letter to indicate enclosures since it will be obvious to the reader that there are enclosures in the envelope

20. Standard rules for typing spacing have developed through usage. 20.___
    According to these rules, one space is left AFTER
    A. a comma
    B. every sentence
    C. a colon
    D. an opening parenthesis

KEY (CORRECT ANSWERS)

1. C	11. D
2. D	12. C
3. B	13. B
4. A	14. A
5. C	15. D
6. A	16. A
7. B	17. B
8. C	18. D
9. A	19. C
10. B	20. A

EXAMINATION SECTION

TEST 1

DIRECTIONS: Each question or incomplete statement is followed by several suggested answers or completions. Select the one that BEST answers the question or completes the statement. *PRINT THE LETTER OF THE CORRECT ANSWER IN THE SPACE AT THE RIGHT.*

1. If you open a personal letter by mistake, the one of the following actions which it would generally be BEST for you to take is to 1.___
   A. ignore your error, attach the envelope to the letter, and distribute in the usual manner
   B. personally give the addressee the letter without any explanation
   C. place the letter inside the envelope, indicate under your initials that it was opened in error, and give to the addressee
   D. reseal the envelope or place the contents in another envelope and pass on to addressee

2. If you receive a telephone call regarding a matter which your office does not handle, you should FIRST 2.___
   A. give the caller the telephone number of the proper office so that he can dial again
   B. offer to transfer the caller to the proper office
   C. suggest that the caller re-dial since he probably dialed incorrectly
   D. tell the caller he has reached the wrong office and then hang up

3. When you answer the telephone, the MOST important reason for identifying yourself and your organization is to 3.___
   A. give the caller time to collect his or her thoughts
   B. impress the caller with your courtesy
   C. inform the caller that he or she has reached the right number
   D. set a business-like tone at the beginning of the conversation

4. The one of the following cases in which you would NOT place a special notation in the left margin of a letter that you have typed is when 4.___
   A. one of the carbon copies is intended for someone other than the addressee of the letter
   B. you enclose a flyer with the letter
   C. you sign your superior's name to the letter, at his or her request
   D. the letter refers to something being sent under separate cover

5. Suppose that you accidentally cut a letter or enclosure as you are opening an envelope with a paper knife. The one of the following that you should do FIRST is to 5.___
   A. determine whether the document is important
   B. clip or staple the pieces together and process as usual
   C. mend the cut document with transparent tape
   D. notify the sender that the communication was damaged and request another copy

6. As soon as you pick up the phone, a very angry caller begins immediately to complain about city agencies and *red tape*. He says that he has been shifted to two or three different offices. It turns out that he is seeking information which is not immediately available to you. You believe you know, however, where it can be found. Which of the following actions is the BEST one for you to take? 6.___
   A. To eliminate all confusion, suggest that the caller write the mayor stating explicitly what he wants.
   B. Apologize by telling the caller how busy city agencies now are, but also tell him directly that you do not have the information he needs.
   C. Ask for the caller's telephone number, and assure him you will call back after you have checked further.
   D. Give the caller the name and telephone number of the person who might be able to help, but explain that you are not positive he will get results.

7. Suppose that one of your duties is to dictate responses to routine requests from the public for information. A letter writer asks for information which, as expressed in a one-sentence, explicit agency rule, cannot be given out to the public. Of the following ways of answering the letter, which is the MOST efficient? 7.___
   A. Quote verbatim that section of the agency rules which prohibits giving this information to the public.
   B. Without quoting the rule, explain why you cannot accede to the request and suggest alternative sources.
   C. Describe how carefully the request was considered before classifying it as subject to the rule forbidding the issuance of such information.
   D. Acknowledge receipt of the letter and advise that the requested information is not released to the public.

8. Suppose you assist in supervising a staff which has rather high morale, and your own supervisor asks you to poll the staff to find out who will be able to work overtime this particular evening to help complete emergency work. 8.___
Which of the following approaches would be MOST likely to win their cooperation while maintaining their morale?
   A. Tell them that the better assignments will be given only to those who work overtime.
   B. Tell them that occasional overtime is a job requirement.
   C. Assure them they'll be doing you a personal favor.
   D. Let them know clearly why the overtime is needed.

9. Suppose that you have been asked to write and to prepare for reproduction new departmental vacation leave regulations. 9.___
After you have written the new regulations, all of which fit on one page, which one of the following would be the BEST method of reproducing 1,000 copies?
   A. An outside private printer because you can best maintain confidentiality using this technique
   B. Xeroxing because the copies will have the best possible appearance
   C. Typing carbon copies because you will be certain that there are the fewest possible errors
   D. The multilith process because it is quick and neat

10. You are in charge of verifying employees' qualifications. This involves telephoning previous employers and schools. One of the applications which you are reviewing contains information which you are almost certain is correct on the basis of what the employee has told you. 10.___
The BEST thing to do is to
   A. check the information again with the employer
   B. perform the required verification procedures
   C. accept the information as valid
   D. ask a superior to verify the information

11. The practice of immediately identifying oneself and one's place of employment when contacting persons on the telephone is 11.___
   A. *good* because the receiver of the call can quickly identify the caller and establish a frame of reference
   B. *good* because it helps to set the caller at ease with the other party
   C. *poor* because it is not necessary to divulge that information when making general calls
   D. *poor* because it takes longer to arrive at the topic to be discussed

12. Which one of the following should be the MOST important overall consideration when preparing a recommendation to automate a large-scale office activity? 12.___
The
   A. number of models of automated equipment available
   B. benefits and costs of automation
   C. fears and resistance of affected employees
   D. experience of offices which have automated similar activities

13. A tickler file is MOST appropriate for filing materials 13.___
   A. chronologically according to date they were received
   B. alphabetically by name
   C. alphabetically by subject
   D. chronologically according to date they should be followed up

14. Which of the following is the BEST reason for decentralizing rather then centralizing the use of duplicating machines? 14.___
   A. Developing and retaining efficient duplicating machine operators
   B. Facilitating supervision of duplicating services
   C. Motivating employees to produce legible duplicated copies
   D. Placing the duplicating machines where they are most convenient and most frequently used

15. Window envelopes are sometimes considered preferable to individually addressed envelopes PRIMARILY because 15.___
   A. window envelopes are available in standard sizes for all purposes
   B. window envelopes are more attractive and official-looking
   C. the use of window envelopes eliminates the risk of inserting a letter in the wrong envelope
   D. the use of window envelopes requires neater typing

16. In planning the layout of a new office, the utilization of space and the arrangement of staff, furnishings, and equipment should usually be MOST influenced by the 16.___
   A. gross square footage
   B. status differences in the chain of command
   C. framework of informal relationships among employees
   D. activities to be performed

17. Office forms sometimes consist of several copies, each of a different color. 17.___
The MAIN reason for using different colors is to
   A. make a favorable impression on the users of the form
   B. distinguish each copy from the others
   C. facilitate the preparation of legible carbon copies
   D. reduce cost, since using colored stock permits recycling of paper

18. Which of the following is the BEST justification for obtaining a photocopying machine for the office? 18.___
   A. A photocopying machine can produce an unlimited number of copies at a low fixed cost per copy.
   B. Employees need little training in operating a photocopying machine.
   C. Office costs will be reduced and efficiency increased.
   D. The legibility of a photocopy generally is superior to copy produced by any other office duplicating device.

19. An administrative officer in charge of a small fund for buying office supplies has just written a check to Charles Laird, a supplier, and has sent the check by messenger to him. A half-hour later, the messenger telephones the administrative officer. He has lost the check. 19.___
Which of the following is the MOST important action for the administrative officer to take under these circumstances?
   A. Ask the messenger to return and write a report describing the loss of the check.
   B. Make a note on the performance record of the messenger who lost the check.
   C. Take the necessary steps to have payment stopped on the check.
   D. Refrain from doing anything since the check may be found shortly.

20. A petty cash fund is set up PRIMARILY to 20.___
   A. take care of small investments that must be made from time to time
   B. take care of small expenses that arise from time to time
   C. provide a fund to be used as the office wants to use it with little need to maintain records
   D. take care of expenses that develop during emergencies such as machine breakdowns and fires

21. Your superior has asked you to send a telegram from your agency to a government agency in another city. He has written out the message and has indicated the name of the government agency. 21.___
When you dictate the message to Western Union, which of the following items that your superior has not mentioned must you be SURE to include?
   A. Today's date
   B. The full address of the government agency
   C. A polite opening such as *Dear Sirs*
   D. A final sentence such as *We would appreciate hearing from your agency in reply as soon as is convenient for you*

22. In addition to the original piece of correspondence, one should USUALLY also have typed 22.___
   A. a single copy
   B. as many copies as can be typed at one time
   C. no more copies than are needed
   D. two copies

23. The one of the following which is the BEST procedure to follow when making a short insert in a completed dictation is to 23.___
   A. label the insert with a letter and indicate the position of the insert in the text by writing the identifying letter in the proper place
   B. squeeze the insert into its proper place within the main text of the dictation
   C. take down the insert and check the placement with the person who dictated when you are ready to transcribe your notes
   D. transcribe the dictation into longhand, including the insert in its proper position

24. The one of the following procedures which will be MOST efficient in helping you to quickly open your dictation notebook to a clean sheet is to 24.___
   A. clip or place a rubberband around the used portion of the notebook
   B. leave the book out and open to a clean page when not in use
   C. transcribe each dictation after it is given and rip out the used pages
   D. use a book marker to indicate which portion of the notebook has been used

25. The purpose of dating your dictation notebooks is GENERALLY to 25.___
   A. enable you to easily refer to your notes at a later date
   B. insure that you transcribe your notes in the order in which they were dictated
   C. set up a precise record-keeping procedure
   D. show your employer that you pay attention to detail

KEY (CORRECT ANSWERS)

1. C	6. C	11. A	16. D	21. B
2. B	7. A	12. B	17. B	22. C
3. C	8. D	13. D	18. C	23. A
4. C	9. D	14. D	19. C	24. A
5. C	10. B	15. C	20. B	25. A

TEST 2

DIRECTIONS: Each question or incomplete statement is followed by several suggested answers or completions. Select the one that BEST answers the question or completes the statement. *PRINT THE LETTER OF THE CORRECT ANSWER IN THE SPACE AT THE RIGHT.*

1. With regard to typed correspondence received by most offices, which of the following is the GREATEST problem? 1.___
   A. Verbosity B. Illegibility
   C. Improper folding D. Excessive copies

2. Of the following, the GREATEST advantage of electric typewriters over manual typewriters is that they usually 2.___
   A. are less expensive to repair
   B. are smaller and lighter
   C. produce better looking copy
   D. require less training for the typist

3. Suppose that a large quantity of information is in the files which are located a good distance from your desk. Almost every worker in your office must use these files constantly. Your duties in particular require that you daily refer to about 25 of the same items. They are short, one-page items distributed throughout the files. In this situation, your BEST course would be to 3.___
   A. take the items that you use daily from the files and keep them on your desk, inserting *out cards* in their place
   B. go to the files each time you need the information so that the items will be there when other workers need them
   C. make xerox copies of the information you use most frequently and keep them in your desk for ready reference
   D. label the items you use most often with different colored tabs for immediate identification

4. Of the following, the MOST important advantage of preparing manuals of office procedures in loose-leaf form is that this form 4.___
   A. permits several employees to use different sections simultaneously
   B. facilitates the addition of new material and the removal of obsolete material
   C. is more readily arranged in alphabetical order
   D. reduces the need for cross-references to locate material carried under several headings

5. Suppose that you establish a new clerical procedure for the unit you supervise. 5.___
Your keeping a close check on the time required by your staff to handle the new procedure is WISE mainly because such a check will find out
   A. whether your subordinates know how to handle the new procedure
   B. whether a revision of the unit's work schedule will be necessary as a result of the new procedure
   C. what attitude your employees have toward the new procedure
   D. what alterations in job descriptions will be necessitated by the new procedure

6. The numbered statements below relate to the stenographic skill of taking dictation. According to authorities on secretarial practices, which of these are generally recommended guides to development of efficient stenographic skills? 6.___

STATEMENTS

1. A stenographer should date her notebook daily to facilitate locating certain notes at a later time.
2. A stenographer should make corrections of grammatical mistakes while her boss is dictating to her.
3. A stenographer should draw a line through the dictated matter in her notebook after she has transcribed it.
4. A stenographer should write in longhand unfamiliar names and addresses dictated to her.

The CORRECT answer is:
   A. Only Statements 1, 2, and 3 are generally recommended guides.
   B. Only Statements 2, 3, and 4 are generally recommended guides.
   C. Only Statements 1, 3, and 4 are generally recommended guides.
   D. All four statements are generally recommended guides.

7. According to generally recognized rules of filing in an alphabetic filing system, the one of the following names which normally should be filed LAST is 7.___
   A. Department of Education, New York State
   B. F.B.I.
   C. Police Department of New York City
   D. P.S. 81 of New York City

8. Which one of the following forms for the typed name of the dictator in the closing lines of a letter is generally MOST acceptable in the United States? 8.___
   A. (Dr.) James F. Fenton
   B. Dr. James F. Fenton
   C. Mr. James F. Fenton, Ph.D.
   D. James F. Fenton

9. Which of the following is, MOST generally, a rule to be followed when typing a rough draft? 9.___
   A. The copy should be single spaced.
   B. The copy should be triple spaced.
   C. There is no need for including footnotes.
   D. Errors must be neatly corrected.

10. An office assistant needs a synonym. 10.___
    Of the following, the book which she would find MOST useful is
    A. a world atlas
    B. BARTLETT'S FAMILIAR QUOTATIONS
    C. a manual of style
    D. a thesaurus

11. Of the following examples of footnotes, the one that is expressed in the MOST generally accepted standard form is: 11.___
    A. Johnson, T.F. (Dr.), English for Everyone, 3rd or 4th edition; New York City Linton Publishing Company, p. 467
    B. Frank Taylor, English for Today (New York: Rayton Publishing Company, 1971), p. 156
    C. Ralph Wilden, English for Tomorrow, Reynolds Publishing Company, England. p. 451
    D. Quinn, David, Yesterday's English (New York: Baldwin Publishing Company, 1972), p. 431

12. Standard procedures are used in offices PRIMARILY because 12.___
    A. an office is a happier place if everyone is doing the tasks in the same manner
    B. particular ways of doing jobs are considered more efficient than other ways
    C. it is good discipline for workers to follow standard procedures approved by the supervisor
    D. supervisors generally don't want workers to be creative in planning their work

13. Assume that an office assistant has the responsibility for compiling, typing, and mailing a preliminary announcement of Spring term , course offerings. The announcement will go to approximately 900 currently enrolled students. Assuming that the following equipment is available for use, the MOST appropriate choice for use in making duplicate copies is generally a 13.___
    A. stencil duplicator
    B. spirit (fluid) duplicator
    C. magnetic card or tape selectric typewriter
    D. copier (Xerox, etc.)

14. *Justified typing* is a term that refers MOST specifically to typewriting copy 14.___
    A. that has been edited and for which final copy is being prepared
    B. in a form that allows for an even right-hand margin

C. with a predetermined vertical placement for each alternate line
D. that has been approved by the supervisor and his superior

15. Which one of the following is the BEST form for the address in a letter? 15.___
A. Mr. John Jones
Vice President, The Universal Printing Company
1220 Fifth Avenue
New York, 10023 New York
B. Mr. John Jones, Vice President
The Universal Printing Company
1220 Fifth Avenue
New York, New York 10023
C. Mr. John Jones, Vice President, The Universal Printing Company
1220 Fifth Avenue
New York, New York 10023
D. Mr. John Jones
Vice President,
The Universal Printing Company
1220 Fifth Avenue
New York, 10023 New York

16. Of the following, the CHIEF advantage of the use of window envelopes over ordinary envelopes is that window envelopes 16.___
A. eliminate the need for addressing envelopes
B. protect the confidential nature of enclosed material
C. cost less to buy than ordinary envelopes
D. reduce the danger of the address becoming illegible

17. In the complimentary close of a business letter, the FIRST letter of ______ should be capitalized. 17.___
A. all the words
B. none of the words
C. only the first word
D. only the last word

18. Assume that one of your duties is to procure needed office supplies from the supply room. You are permitted to draw supplies every two weeks. 18.___
The one of the following which would be the MOST desirable practice for you to follow in obtaining supplies is to
A. obtain a quantity of supplies sufficient to last for several months to make certain that enough supplies are always on hand
B. determine the minimum supply which it is necessary to keep on hand for the various items and obtain an additional quantity as soon as possible after the supply on hand has been reduced to this minimum
C. review the supplies once a month to determine what items have been exhausted and obtain an additional quantity as soon as possible
D. obtain a supply of an item as soon after it has been exhausted as is possible

19. Some offices that keep carbon copies of letters use several different colors of carbon paper for making carbon copies. 19.___
Of the following, the CHIEF reason for using different colors of carbon paper is to
A. facilitate identification of different types of letters in the files
B. relieve the monotony of typing and filing carbon copies
C. reduce the costs of preparing carbon copies
D. utilize both sides of the carbon paper for typing

20. If 20,000 copies of a form are to be reproduced, the one of the following types of duplicating machines that would be the MOST suitable one to use is the 20.___
A. mimeograph B. photocopy
C. multilith D. ditto

21. Gary Thompson is applying for a position with the firm of Gray and Williams. 21.___
Which letter should be filed in top position in the *Application* folder?
A. A letter of recommendation written on September 18 by Johnson & Smith
B. Williams' letter of October 8 requesting further details regarding Thompson's experience
C. Thompson's letter of September 8 making application for a position as sales manager
D. Letter of September 20 from Alfred Jackson recommending Thompson for the job

22. The USUAL arrangement in indexing the names of the First National Bank, Toledo, is 22.___
A. First National Bank, Toledo, Ohio
B. Ohio, First National Bank, Toledo
C. Toledo, First National Bank, Ohio
D. Ohio, Toledo, First National Bank

23. To disengage the mechanism so that the carriage can move freely from side to side, use the 23.___
A. paper release
B. margin release
C. variable line space lever
D. carriage release

24. To center an article that requires 50 typed lines on paper $8\frac{1}{2}$ x 13, the FIRST line should be started ____ spaces below top edge. 24.___
A. 8 B. 14 C. 17 D. 25

25. The subject line in a letter is USUALLY typed a _____ space below the _____. 25.___
A. single; inside address B. single; salutation
C. double; inside address D. double; salutation

KEY (CORRECT ANSWERS)

1. A
2. C
3. C
4. B
5. B

6. C
7. B
8. D
9. B
10. D

11. B
12. B
13. A
14. B
15. B

16. A
17. C
18. B
19. A
20. C

21. B
22. C
23. D
24. B
25. D

EXAMINATION SECTION

DIRECTIONS: Each question or incomplete statement is followed by several suggested answers or completions. Select the one that BEST answers the question or completes the statement. *PRINT THE LETTER OF THE CORRECT ANSWER IN THE SPACE AT THE RIGHT.*

1. In considering a new word processing system for a regional office, which of the following would MOST likely be the MOST important consideration in making a decision? 1.___
   A. Ease of operation
   B. Friendliness of service technicians
   C. Availability of service technicians
   D. Capacity of the system to meet the unit's word processing needs

2. Your supervisor is out of town for several days and has asked you to act as supervisor in his absence. An employee in the unit comes to you and complains that the supervisor has been dividing the workload unfairly. 2.___
   Of the following, the MOST appropriate action for you to take is
   A. defend the actions of your supervisor
   B. encourage the employee to file a grievance
   C. listen to the employee attentively
   D. explain to the employee that you have no authority to handle the situation

3. A principal stenographer still on probation is instructed to supervise and coordinate the completion of a large word processing project. Her supervisor asks her how long she thinks the project will take. The principal stenographer gives her supervisor an estimate that is two days longer than she actually thinks the project will take to complete. The project is completed two days earlier, and the principal stenographer is congratulated by her supervisor for her efforts. 3.___
   In purposely overestimating the time required to complete the project, the principal stenographer showed
   A. *good* judgment because it helped her appear very efficient
   B. *good* judgment because it helps keep unrealistic supervisors from expecting too much
   C. *poor* judgment because plans and schedules of other components of the project may have been based on her false estimate
   D. *poor* judgment because she should have used the extra time to further check and proofread the work

4. Which of the following would MOST likely be the MOST important in providing support to one's supervisor? 4.___
   A. Screening annoying phone calls
   B. Reviewing and forwarding articles and publications that may be of interest to your supervisor
   C. Correctly transmitting instructions from the supervisor to appropriate staff members
   D. Reviewing outgoing correspondence for proper grammatical usage and clarity

5. While you are on the telephone answering a question about your agency, a visitor comes to your desk and starts to ask you a question. There is no emergency or urgency in either situation, that of the phone call or that of answering the visitor's question. 5.___
   In this case, you should
   A. excuse yourself to the person on the telephone and tell the visitor that you will be with him or her as soon as you have finished on the phone
   B. explain to the person on the phone that you have a visitor and must shorten the conversation
   C. continue to talk with the person on the phone while looking up occasionally at the visitor to let him or her know that you know he or she is there
   D. continue to talk with the person on the telephone until you are finished and then let the visitor know that you're sorry to have kept him or her waiting

6. Your supervisor is out of town on vacation for one week, and asks you to act as supervisor in her absence. The second day she is gone a very important, complex budgetary form, which must be responded to in ten days, arrives in your unit. 6.___
   Of the following, it would be BEST if you
   A. filled out the form and submitted it as soon as possible
   B. read the form over, did any time-consuming research that might be needed, and then gave the uncompleted form to your supervisor as soon as she returned
   C. asked for help from your supervisor's supervisor in completing the form
   D. tried to contact your supervisor for advice

7. Of the following, which would MOST likely be of the highest priority? 7.___
   The typing of
   A. a grant proposal due next week
   B. new addresses onto a mailing list for a future mailing
   C. a payroll form for a new employee that needs to be submitted immediately
   D. a memorandum from the Commissioner to all employees regarding new procedures

8. Your office is moving to a new location. 8.____
Of the following, it would be MOST important to ensure that
   A. others will know your office's new address and phone number
   B. the new office space is comfortable
   C. your supervisor is happy with his or her new office space
   D. the move itself goes smoothly

9. Of the following, which would generally be considered the LEAST desirable? 9.____
   A. Accidentally disconnecting an executive from an important phone call
   B. Ordering the wrong back-up part for a copying machine
   C. Misplacing several hundred dollars worth of personal checks payable to your department
   D. Misplacing a memorandum that needs to be typed

10. Your supervisor has told you not to let anyone disturb her for the rest of the morning unless absolutely necessary because she has some urgent work to complete. The department head telephones and asks to speak to her. 10.____
The BEST course of action for you to take is to
   A. ask the department head if he or she can leave a message
   B. ask your supervisor if she can take the call
   C. tell the department head that your supervisor is out
   D. let your supervisor know that her instructions have put you in a difficult position

11. Which of the following would be MOST likely to contribute to efficiency in the operation of an office? 11.____
   A. A new computer system is instituted in an office.
   B. The employees are paid well.
   C. Procedures and practices are studied for any redundant operations.
   D. A supervisor delegates work.

12. You are at work at your desk on a special project when a visitor approaches you. You cannot interrupt your work to take care of this person. 12.____
Of the following, the BEST and MOST courteous way of handling this situation is to
   A. avoid looking up from your work until you are finished with what you are doing
   B. tell the visitor that you will not be able to assist him or her for quite some time
   C. refer the individual to another employee who can take care of him or her right away
   D. chat with the individual while you continue to work

13. Which of the following would MOST likely be of the highest priority? 13.___
A(n)
   A. annual report due next month
   B. irate member of the public who is standing at your desk
   C. important financial report requested by the Commissioner
   D. memorandum to all employees outlining very important new policy needs to be typed and distributed immediately

14. Someone uses *special pull* to obtain the services of your unit at the last minute. You and the four employees you supervise have done everything you could do to provide good service, and you feel things have gone very well. The client is not pleased, however, and enters your office and begins screaming at you and the other employees present. 14.___
Of the following, it would be BEST if you
   A. ignored the person
   B. tried to calm the person down
   C. asked the person to leave the office
   D. called your supervisor in to help handle the situation

15. Your supervisor is on vacation for two weeks, and you have been asked to fill in for her. Your office is very busy, and there is a strict procedure for filling requests. Leslie from Unit X wants something completed immediately. You don't feel this is possible or reasonable, and politely explain why to Leslie. Leslie becomes very angry and says that she will complain to your supervisor about your uncooperative behavior as soon as your supervisor returns. 15.___
Of the following, it would be BEST if you
   A. filled Leslie's request
   B. reported Leslie to her supervisor
   C. complained to your supervisor about the situation as soon as she returned
   D. stood by your decision once you determined it was correct

---

KEY (CORRECT ANSWERS)

1. D	6. B	11. C
2. C	7. C	12. C
3. C	8. A	13. B
4. C	9. C	14. B
5. A	10. B	15. D

EXAMINATION SECTION

DIRECTIONS: Each question or incomplete statement is followed by several suggested answers or completions. Select the one that BEST answers the question or completes the statement. *PRINT THE LETTER OF THE CORRECT ANSWER IN THE SPACE AT THE RIGHT.*

1. In considering a new word processing system for a regional office, which of the following would MOST likely be the MOST important consideration in making a decision? 1.___
   A. Ease of operation
   B. Friendliness of service technicians
   C. Availability of service technicians
   D. Capacity of the system to meet the unit's word processing needs

2. Your supervisor is out of town for several days and has asked you to act as supervisor in his absence. An employee in the unit comes to you and complains that the supervisor has been dividing the workload unfairly. 2.___
   Of the following, the MOST appropriate action for you to take is
   A. defend the actions of your supervisor
   B. encourage the employee to file a grievance
   C. listen to the employee attentively
   D. explain to the employee that you have no authority to handle the situation

3. A principal stenographer still on probation is instructed to supervise and coordinate the completion of a large word processing project. Her supervisor asks her how long she thinks the project will take. The principal stenographer gives her supervisor an estimate that is two days longer than she actually thinks the project will take to complete. The project is completed two days earlier, and the principal stenographer is congratulated by her supervisor for her efforts. 3.___
   In purposely overestimating the time required to complete the project, the principal stenographer showed
   A. *good* judgment because it helped her appear very efficient
   B. *good* judgment because it helps keep unrealistic supervisors from expecting too much
   C. *poor* judgment because plans and schedules of other components of the project may have been based on her false estimate
   D. *poor* judgment because she should have used the extra time to further check and proofread the work

4. Which of the following would MOST likely be the MOST important in providing support to one's supervisor? 4.___
   A. Screening annoying phone calls
   B. Reviewing and forwarding articles and publications that may be of interest to your supervisor
   C. Correctly transmitting instructions from the supervisor to appropriate staff members
   D. Reviewing outgoing correspondence for proper grammatical usage and clarity

5. While you are on the telephone answering a question about your agency, a visitor comes to your desk and starts to ask you a question. There is no emergency or urgency in either situation, that of the phone call or that of answering the visitor's question. 5.___
   In this case, you should
   A. excuse yourself to the person on the telephone and tell the visitor that you will be with him or her as soon as you have finished on the phone
   B. explain to the person on the phone that you have a visitor and must shorten the conversation
   C. continue to talk with the person on the phone while looking up occasionally at the visitor to let him or her know that you know he or she is there
   D. continue to talk with the person on the telephone until you are finished and then let the visitor know that you're sorry to have kept him or her waiting

6. Your supervisor is out of town on vacation for one week, and asks you to act as supervisor in her absence. The second day she is gone a very important, complex budgetary form, which must be responded to in ten days, arrives in your unit. 6.___
   Of the following, it would be BEST if you
   A. filled out the form and submitted it as soon as possible
   B. read the form over, did any time-consuming research that might be needed, and then gave the uncompleted form to your supervisor as soon as she returned
   C. asked for help from your supervisor's supervisor in completing the form
   D. tried to contact your supervisor for advice

7. Of the following, which would MOST likely be of the highest priority? 7.___
   The typing of
   A. a grant proposal due next week
   B. new addresses onto a mailing list for a future mailing
   C. a payroll form for a new employee that needs to be submitted immediately
   D. a memorandum from the Commissioner to all employees regarding new procedures

8. Your office is moving to a new location. 8.___
Of the following, it would be MOST important to ensure that
   A. others will know your office's new address and phone number
   B. the new office space is comfortable
   C. your supervisor is happy with his or her new office space
   D. the move itself goes smoothly

9. Of the following, which would generally be considered the LEAST desirable? 9.___
   A. Accidentally disconnecting an executive from an important phone call
   B. Ordering the wrong back-up part for a copying machine
   C. Misplacing several hundred dollars worth of personal checks payable to your department
   D. Misplacing a memorandum that needs to be typed

10. Your supervisor has told you not to let anyone disturb her for the rest of the morning unless absolutely necessary because she has some urgent work to complete. The department head telephones and asks to speak to her. 10.___
The BEST course of action for you to take is to
   A. ask the department head if he or she can leave a message
   B. ask your supervisor if she can take the call
   C. tell the department head that your supervisor is out
   D. let your supervisor know that her instructions have put you in a difficult position

11. Which of the following would be MOST likely to contribute to efficiency in the operation of an office? 11.___
   A. A new computer system is instituted in an office.
   B. The employees are paid well.
   C. Procedures and practices are studied for any redundant operations.
   D. A supervisor delegates work.

12. You are at work at your desk on a special project when a visitor approaches you. You cannot interrupt your work to take care of this person. 12.___
Of the following, the BEST and MOST courteous way of handling this situation is to
   A. avoid looking up from your work until you are finished with what you are doing
   B. tell the visitor that you will not be able to assist him or her for quite some time
   C. refer the individual to another employee who can take care of him or her right away
   D. chat with the individual while you continue to work

13. Which of the following would MOST likely be of the highest priority? 13.___
A(n)
A. annual report due next month
B. irate member of the public who is standing at your desk
C. important financial report requested by the Commissioner
D. memorandum to all employees outlining very important new policy needs to be typed and distributed immediately

14. Someone uses *special pull* to obtain the services of your unit at the last minute. You and the four employees you supervise have done everything you could do to provide good service, and you feel things have gone very well. The client is not pleased, however, and enters your office and begins screaming at you and the other employees present. 14.___
Of the following, it would be BEST if you
A. ignored the person
B. tried to calm the person down
C. asked the person to leave the office
D. called your supervisor in to help handle the situation

15. Your supervisor is on vacation for two weeks, and you have been asked to fill in for her. Your office is very busy, and there is a strict procedure for filling requests. Leslie from Unit X wants something completed immediately. You don't feel this is possible or reasonable, and politely explain why to Leslie. Leslie becomes very angry and says that she will complain to your supervisor about your uncooperative behavior as soon as your supervisor returns. 15.___
Of the following, it would be BEST if you
A. filled Leslie's request
B. reported Leslie to her supervisor
C. complained to your supervisor about the situation as soon as she returned
D. stood by your decision once you determined it was correct

KEY (CORRECT ANSWERS)

1. D	6. B	11. C
2. C	7. C	12. C
3. C	8. A	13. B
4. C	9. C	14. B
5. A	10. B	15. D

EXAMINATION SECTION

TEST 1

DIRECTIONS: Each question or incomplete statement is followed by several suggested answers or completions. Select the one that BEST answers the question or completes the statement. *PRINT THE LETTER OF THE CORRECT ANSWER IN THE SPACE AT THE RIGHT.*

ABBREVIATIONS

DIRECTIONS: Write the meaning of the following abbreviations.

1. cm. 1.___
2. mdse. 2.___
3. O.R. 3.___
4. Fwd. 4.___
5. ex div. 5.___
6. k 6.___
7. pro tem 7.___
8. XXXX 8.___
9. sine die 9.___
10. pk. 10.___
11. ea. 11.___
12. G/A 12.___
13. execx. 13.___
14. c.w.o. 14.___
15. ad val. 15.___

TEST 2

BUSINESS INFORMATION

DIRECTIONS: Indicate the CORRECT answer for the following questions.

1. A ream of 24-lb. paper 8½ x 11 will weigh APPROXIMATELY _____ lbs. 1.___

2. The escapement of the typewriter is the part that controls the _____. 2.___

3. The device MOST useful in making a freehand drawing on a stencil is a(n) _____. 3.___

4. The typist uses the _____ to make an exact adjustment of lined paper to the horizontal writing position. 4.___

5. The duplicating process in which the master copy is formed in reverse by inserting the carbon paper face up is known as _____. 5.___

6. Ball point, Wheel, and Needle-point all refer to _____. 6.___

7. If the impression paper as it is ejected from the duplicating machines does NOT drop quickly and in orderly fashion, the trouble is usually due to _____. 7.___

8. This may USUALLY be eliminated by the use of a(n) _____. 8.___

9. The copy recorder for Xerox 5090, 9900, and 9500 will count a MAXIMUM of _____ copies at one setting. 9.___

10. A *half back-space* key is standard on the _____. 10.___

11. The process of making typewritten or printed lines even in length or special spacing is known as _____. 11.___

12. Standard size letterheads are _____ inches in size. 12.___

13. The size of type currently in common use on the typewriter is known as _____. 13.___

14. It measures _____ typing spaces to an inch (horizontal). 14.___

15. Another popular type size is the _____. 15.___

16. Which measures _____ typing spaces to an inch (horizontal). 16.___

17. The two parts of a letter omitted in interoffice communi- 17.___
18. cations are _____ and _____. 18.___

19. A first-class letter weighing 3½ ounces is sent with 88 cents affixed in stamps. 19.___
Assuming 1st class postage is 29¢, postage due is _____.

20. An air-mail letter weighing one-half ounce requires _____ postage. 20.___

21. Offset, Bristol, Cover, Ledger - all refer to _____. 21.___

22. The three items of information USUALLY placed at the 22.___
23. top of the second page of a letter are _____, _____. 23.___
24. and _____. 24.___

25. When typing printed copy in italics, the _____ is used to indicate the italicized words. 25.___

TEST 3

LITERATURE

DIRECTIONS: Each question or incomplete statement is followed by several suggested answers or completions. Select the one that BEST answers the question or completes the statement. *PRINT THE LETTER OF THE CORRECT ANSWER IN THE SPACE AT THE RIGHT.*

1. THE LADY OR THE TIGER by Frank R. Stockton 1.___
   A. is a story of hunting in Asia
   B. ends with the marriage of the youth
   C. ends with a dilemma
   D. ends with the lady inside the tiger

2. A teacher planning an assembly program in commemoration of Abraham Lincoln would find the MOST appropriate material about Lincoln in the poetry of 2.___
   A. Edna St. Vincent Millay B. Rudyard Kipling
   C. Walt Whitman D. James Whitcomb Riley

3. *To thine own self be true*
   And it will follow as the night the day
   Thou can'st not then be false to any man
   is a quotation from 3.___
   A. the Bible B. Shakespeare
   C. the IDYLLS OF THE KING D. Benjamin Franklin

4. Of the following, the one who is NOT a poet is 4.___
   A. Arthur Guiterman B. Robert Frost
   C. John Masefield D. Joseph C. Lincoln

5. Captain Hook is a character in 5.___
   A. TREASURE ISLAND B. NORTHWEST PASSAGE
   C. PETER PAN D. CAPTAINS COURAGEOUS

6. *God's in His heaven*
   All's right with the world
   was spoken by a(n) 6.___
   A. Southern slave
   B. dying Confederate soldier
   C. Italian child factory worker
   D. shipwrecked mariner

7. Hans Christian Andersen did NOT write THE 7.___
   A. STEADFAST TIN SOLDIER
   B. EMPEROR'S NEW CLOTHES
   C. KING OF THE GOLDEN RIVER
   D. UGLY DUCKLING

8. In the PIED PIPER OF HAMELIN, Browning implies that 8.___
   A. birds of a feather flock together
   B. necessity is the mother of invention
   C. honesty is the best policy
   D. fine feathers do not make fine birds

9. *And they shall beat their swords into ploughshares, and their spears into pruning-hooks; nation shall not lift up sword against nation, neither shall they learn war any more* is a quotation from 9.___
   A. Ruskin   B. Tolstoy   C. Carlyle   D. the Bible

10. *He prayeth best who loveth best*
All things both great and small,
For the dear God who loveth us
is completed by Coleridge with the line 10.___
   A. Is Father of us all
   B. He loveth great and small
   C. Doth mark the sparrow's fall
   D. He made and loveth all

11. *This is the forest primeval. The murmuring pines and the hemlocks, Bearded with moss, and in garments green, indistinct in the twilight Stand like Druids of old...* are lines from 11.___
   A. EVANGELINE
   B. THE SINGING LEAVES
   C. THE BALLAD OF EAST AND WEST
   D. HIAWATHA

12. *What is that which the breeze o'er the towering steep,*
As it fitfully blows, half conceals half discloses?
Now it catches the gleam of the morning's first beam,
In full glory reflected now shines on the stream.
These lines are from THE 12.___
   A. AMERICAN FLAG - J.R. Drake
   B. STAR-SPANGLED BANNER - F.S. Key
   C. NAME OF OLD GLORY - J.W. Riley
   D. BUGLE SONG - A. Tennyson

13. Of the following children's stories, the one in which an animal plays the MOST important part is 13.___
   A. HANSEL AND GRETEL   B. SNOW WHITE
   C. FERDINAND   D. THE ROSE AND THE RING

14. *The noblest Roman of them all* was 14.___
   A. Caesar   B. Horatius   C. Antony   D. Brutus

15. Of the following statements, the one which is TRUE concerning the story entitled THE NECKLACE is: 15.___
   A. The borrowed necklace was paste
   B. The borrowed necklace was a diamond necklace worth about 40,000 francs
   C. Madame Loisel did not enjoy the ball at which she wore the necklace
   D. The couple worked almost a year to pay for the lost necklace

16. The TANGLEWOOD TALES are 16.___
A. fairy tales B. nature stories
C. stories from mythology D. essays on music

17. William Tell is a legendary national hero of 17.___
A. Denmark B. Sweden
C. Switzerland D. Austria

18. An American writer who won fame for his stories about Indians is 18.___
A. William Cullen Bryant B. Henry David Thoreau
C. James Fenimore Cooper D. Ralph Waldo Emerson

19. The ghost of Banquo appears in 19.___
A. HAMLET B. JULIUS CAESAR
C. OTHELLO D. MACBETH

20. Odysseus was bound to the mast of the ship when he and his men sailed past 20.___
A. Calypso's Island B. Scylla and Charybdis
C. the Sirens D. the land of the Cyclops

21. All of the following stories are about animals EXCEPT 21.___
A. THE YEARLING B. ZENOBIA'S INFIDELITY
C. THE MONKEY'S PAW D. MY FRIEND FLICKA

22. The poem THE WRECK OF THE HESPERUS tells about 22.___
A. men drifting in a life boat
B. the death of a boatman and his daughter
C. an amusing game played with toy boats
D. the hardships suffered by the crew of a sailing vessel

23. When Gulliver landed on the island of the Lilluputians, the natives rendered him helpless by 23.___
A. offering him drugged wine
B. tying him down with ropes
C. showering him with arrows
D. removing all his clothes

24. POOR RICHARD'S ALMANAC concerns 24.___
A. a boy named Richard
B. wise sayings about life
C. statistics on the weather
D. tramp life

25. According to Poe's account, the raven 25.___
A. perched on a bust of Pallas
B. talked at great length
C. ate cheese from the author's table
D. quickly flew away

TEST 4

PRONUNCIATION

DIRECTIONS: Select the letter of the CORRECT pronunciation.

1. WRESTLING — 1.___
   A. rĕst´ ling B. rās´ ling C. rĕs´ ling

2. JUDICIAL — 2.___
   A. jŭd ĭsh´ al B. jōō dĭsh´ al C. jōō´ dĭsh al

3. EXPERIMENT — 3.___
   A. eks pĕr´ i ment B. eks pēr´ i ment
   C. eks pĕr i ment´

4. SECRETARY — 4.___
   A. sĕk´ re tĕr i B. sēk´ er tĕr i C. sĕk re tĕr´ i

5. MOBILE — 5.___
   A. mō bēl´ B. mō´ bĭl C. mŏ´ bēl

6. AUTOPSY — 6.___
   A. ô´ tŏp si B. ô tŏp´ si C. ō´ tŏp si

7. MINIATURE — 7.___
   A. mĭn´ ĭ ȧ tur B. mĭn ĭ ȧ tur´ C. mĭn ĭ ā´ tur

8. ITALICS — 8.___
   A. ī tăl´ iks B. ī tăl´ iks C. ĭt´ ăl iks

9. INCORRIGIBLE — 9.___
   A. ĭn kōr´ ĭ ji b'l B. ĭn kô rĭj´ i b'l
   C. ĭn kŏr´ ī ji b'l

10. CLICHÉ — 10.___
    A. klĭ kā´ B. klĭsh C. kle shā´

TEST 5

SPELLING

DIRECTIONS: One word in each lettered group is misspelled. Indicate the letter of the misspelled word. *PRINT THE LETTER OF THE CORRECT ANSWER IN THE SPACE AT THE RIGHT.*

1. A. ceremoniously B. desireability C. hazards D. heritage 1.___
2. A. proceeds B. preceding C. supercede D. procedure 2.___
3. A. interoffice B. intrammural C. intestate D. intercede 3.___
4. A. prevaricated B. prefabricate C. chrysantenums D. juxtaposition 4.___
5. A. adjustible B. tangible C. noticeable D. formidable 5.___
6. A. assiduous B. enlightening C. cancellation D. colateral 6.___
7. A. questionnaire B. sacriligious C. mendacious D. fallacious 7.___
8. A. embezzlement B. impanel C. casuality D. subpoena 8.___
9. A. pecuniary B. commissary C. comptroller D. resevoir 9.___
10. A. pramatism B. emphasize C. hyphenize D. hypercritical 10.___
11. A. paragon B. metamorphesis C. collaboration D. colleague 11.___
12. A. aphorism B. benediction C. benignent D. seizure 12.___
13. A. bankrupcy B. coherency C. ascendancy D. truancy 13.___
14. A. withdrawal B. withal C. wearisome D. withold 14.___
15. A. ecrue B. edification C. ecclesiastic D. effluence 15.___

16.	A. accidentally C. grievous	B. remembrance D. sufferage	16.___
17.	A. forfeit C. antidote	B. mischief D. antidate	17.___
18.	A. benefited C. disastrous	B. regretable D. mountainous	18.___
19.	A. perseverance C. preponderence	B. insistence D. recurrence	19.___
20.	A. facetious C. fictitious	B. factitious D. fractous	20.___
21.	A. transmittance C. indubitably	B. undoubtly D. sustenance	21.___
22.	A. appraisor C. auditor	B. creditor D. consignor	22.___
23.	A. mottoes C. soloes	B. pianos D. mementoes	23.___
24.	A. sisters-in-law C. cross-purposes	B. alumini D. 1960's	24.___
25.	A. idiocyncracy C. propeller	B. kimono D. buoyancy	25.___

TEST 6

SYLLABIFICATION

DIRECTIONS: For each word listed below, one correct syllabification is shown. Indicate the CORRECT choice. *PRINT THE LETTER OF THE CORRECT ANSWER IN THE SPACE AT THE RIGHT.*

1. A. rep er cus sion B. re per cus sion 1.___
   C. rep er cuss ion D. re perc us sion
2. A. corr es pon dence B. cor resp on dence 2.___
   C. cor re spond ence D. cor res pond ence
3. A. sup er in ten dent B. su per in ten dent 3.___
   C. su per int end ent D. su per in tend ent
4. A. ac com mo date B. acc om mod ate 4.___
   C. acc omm o date D. ac com mod ate
5. A. ac know ledge B. ac knowl edge 5.___
   C. ack nowl edge D. ack now ledge
6. A. aud it or ium B. au dit or ium 6.___
   C. aud i tor i um D. au di to ri um
7. A. hosp i tal ize B. hos pit a lize 7.___
   C. hosp it al ize D. hos pi tal ize
8. A. du pli ca tion B. dup lic a tion 8.___
   C. du plic a tion D. dup li ca tion
9. A. re cap i tu late B. rec ap it u late 9.___
   C. re ca pi tu late D. re ca pit u late
10. A. com plim en ta ry B. com pli men ta ry 10.___
    C. comp lim ent ar y D. comp li ment a ry

TEST 7

USAGE

DIRECTIONS: In each of the following groups of sentences, there are three sentences which are correct and one which is incorrect because it contains an error in grammar, usage, diction, or punctuation. Indicate the letter of the INCORRECT sentence. *PRINT THE LETTER OF THE CORRECT ANSWER IN THE SPACE AT THE RIGHT.*

1. A. The business was organized under the name of Allen & Co. 1.___
   B. The price of admission was two dollars.
   C. The news was brought to Mr. Walters.
   D. There are less slips to be checked today than there were yesterday.

2. A. He only wants you to go with him; consequently I would be in the way. 2.___
   B. Whom do you think I saw on my way to lunch today?
   C. I am very much pleased with the work you are doing in my office.
   D. I think he is better than anyone else in his class.

3. A. I do not believe in his going so far away from home. 3.___
   B. She dresses exactly like her sister does.
   C. Neither Flora nor I is going to the movies tonight.
   D. The reason for my lateness is that the train was derailed.

4. A. I cannot understand its being on the bottom shelf because I remember putting it on the top shelf. 4.___
   B. If you do not agree with the statement above, please put a check next to it.
   C. We were both chosen to represent the association.
   D. The doctor assured us that she would not have to be operated.

5. A. Near the desk stand three chairs. 5.___
   B. How many crates of oranges were delivered?
   C. Where's your coat and hat?
   D. Either you or your mother is wrong.

6. A. She attacked the proposal with bitter words. 6.___
   B. Last year our team beat your team.
   C. The careless child spilled some milk on the table cloth.
   D. For three weeks last summer, Molly stood with her aunt.

7. A. Don't blame me for it. 7.___
   B. I have met but four.
   C. Loan me five dollars.
   D. May I leave early tonight?

8. A. He was extremely kind to me yesterday. 8.___
B. I talked to him in regard to the subscription.
C. They were so good to me.
D. The teacher spoke clear and emphatic.

9. A. Our vacation is over, I am sorry to say. 9.___
B. It is so dark that I can't hardly see.
C. Either you or I am right; we cannot both be right.
D. After it had lain in the rain all night, it was not fit for use again.

10. A. When either or both habits become fixed, the student improves. 10.___
B. Neither his words nor his action was justifiable.
C. A calm almost always comes before a storm.
D. The gallery with all its pictures were destroyed.

11. A. Next summer I shall either travel by plane or by boat down to Bermuda. 11.___
B. The reason Tom won the award is that he studied hard.
C. Undoubtedly the best scene in the play occurs when the son confronts his mother.
D. History is the record of events that have happened.

12. A. John was invited to spend a week at the camp. 12.___
B. My failure was due to the poor method of study I employed at that time.
C. When I left home, I was only fifteen years old.
D. We imply from your remarks that you think him guilty.

13. A. The advantages of such an arrangement enables the teachers to plan her work more efficiently. 13.___
B. Typing skill is the result merely of the acquisition of a number of habits.
C. We are more likely to catch cold in overheated rooms than in chilly ones.
D. Both political parties promise to balance the budget if and when they are elected to office.

14. A. They have neither the patience nor the skill necessary to solve these problems. 14.___
B. This is the only decision that can be reached: either you or I are right.
C. You should lend your book to the student who you think will enjoy reading it.
D. The Red Cross is doing its utmost to provide medical supplies for the flood areas.

15. A. The driver sustained internal injuries. 15.___
B. It is the only textbook of its kind that has, is, or may be published.
C. Thinking speaking and writing are closely related learnings.
D. Most of us recognize good English when we hear it or read it.

16. A. This sort of emergency always has its exciting moments. 16.___
B. A tragic play is when the action ends unhappily.
C. The committee adjourned sine die and went to their homes for a much needed rest.
D. It is essential that you be on the alert at all times.

17. A. The reason he was late getting to work was because he overslept. 17.___
B. As we read the daily newspaper headlines, a feeling of despair overwhelms us.
C. His gentle speech is no proof that he is kind.
D. Shall we lay the book on the table?

18. A. We want to travel extensively and have new experiences. 18.___
B. Charles is my brother, James being my cousin.
C. His teacher is one person in whom he can confide.
D. The skater suddenly lost control and crashed into the rail.

19. A. Because he was sympathetic and tolerant, most people respected him. 19.___
B. What are the principal points to be emphasized in the conduct of drill practice?
C. The lecturer called attention to the beginning of the movement and how it ended.
D. The average citizen has far more civic power than he realizes.

20. A. The committee has done their best to raise the money necessary to build the new club house. 20.___
B. He was neither willing nor able to pay the exorbitant fee.
C. We all want to be happy, and we want our fellow men to be happy.
D. If ours were a totalitarian society, we would probably limit the number of pupils admitted to colleges.

21. A. The filling-out of the application blank took up one third of his time. 21.___
B. The talent for brevity is given to few politicians!
C. Dashing to the front window, the parade came into view.
D. Each day this newspaper prints a summary of up-to-the-minute news on the front page.

22. A. Because of his ability as a leader, he was undoubtedly the man for the job. 22.___
B. Not only were they disappointed but also angry.
C. If one is to learn French well one must speak it regularly.
D. The most famous collection of prayers known to history is the Book of Psalms.

23. A. We planned to stay a week in at Rocky Landing. 23.___
B. The bus driver agreed to take as many as wanted to go.
C. Any man may vote, be he rich or poor.
D. The teacher assigned three of us, John, Sam, and I, to help with the arrangements for the party.

24. A. It's time you knew how to divide by two numbers. 24.___
B. Are you sure the bell has rung?
C. Whose going to prepare the luncheon?
D. Will it be all right if you are called at ten o'clock?

25. A. He had a wide knowledge of birds. 25.___
B. New Orleans is further from Seattle than from Camden.
C. Keats's poetry is characterized by rich imagery.
D. He objected to several things - the cost, the gaudiness, and the congestion.

TEST 8

VOCABULARY

Questions 1-5.

DIRECTIONS: Write the form ending in ER, OR, or AR.

1. advise 1.___
2. pallid 2.___
3. waive 3.___
4. squalid 4.___
5. defy 5.___

Questions 6-15.

DIRECTIONS: Write the form with prefix meaning NOT.

6. limitable 6.___
7. septic 7.___
8. dispensable 8.___
9. noble 9.___
10. prudent 10.___
11. seasonable 11.___
12. material 12.___
13. reducible 13.___
14. palpable 14.___
15. apt 15.___

Questions 16-20.

DIRECTIONS: Write the form ending in ABLE or IBLE.

16. live 16.___
17. duty 17.___
18. direct 18.___
19. accede 19.___
20. force 20.___

Questions 21-25.

DIRECTIONS: Write the abbreviations for the following.

21. page 21.__
22. pages 22.__
23. namely 23.__
24. for example 24.__
25. which see 25.__

Questions 26-30.

DIRECTIONS: Write the form ending in ERY, ORY, or ARY.

26. machine 26.__
27. mission 27.__
28. promise 28.__
29. distill 29.__
30. provide 30.__

Questions 31-40.

DIRECTIONS: Write the adjective form ending in OUS.

31. mischief 31.__
32. beauty 32.__
33. pretension 33.__
34. scurrility 34.__
35. perspicacity 35.__
36. prodigy 36.__
37. censor 37.__
38. tumult 38.__
39. bounty 39.__
40. merit 40.__

Questions 41-45.

DIRECTIONS: Write the form ending in ANCE, ENCE, or ENTS.

41. abound 41.___

42. cohere 42.___

43. benefit 43.___

44. grief 44.___

45. maintain 45.___

Questions 46-50.

DIRECTIONS: Write the meaning of each abbreviation.

46. ibid. 46.___

47. circa. 47.___

48. vs. 48.___

49. Ms. 49.___

50. cc. 50.___

KEY (CORRECT ANSWERS)

TEST 1
ABBREVIATIONS

1. centimeter
2. merchandise
3. owner's risk
4. forward
5. without dividend
6. carat
7. for the time being
8. best quality
9. without a day for meeting
10. peck
11. each
12. general average
13. executrix
14. cash with order
15. according to value

TEST 2
BUSINESS INFORMATION

1. 6
2. carriage
3. stylus
4. variable line spacer
5. Ditto or Hectograph
6. stylus points
7. static electricity
8. ground wire
9. 9999
10. varityper
11. justifying
12. 8½ x 11
13. elite
14. 10
15. pica
16. 12
17. inside address
18. complimentary close
19. 10¢
20. 29¢
21. paper
22. person addressed
23. page
24. date
25. underscore

TEST 3
LITERATURE

1. C
2. C
3. B
4. D
5. C
6. C
7. C
8. C
9. D
10. D
11. A
12. B
13. C
14. D
15. A
16. C
17. C
18. C
19. D
20. C
21. C
22. B
23. B
24. B
25. A

TEST 4
PRONUNCIATION

1. C
2. B
3. A
4. A
5. B
6. A
7. A
8. A
9. C
10. C

TEST 5
SPELLING

1. B
2. C
3. B
4. C
5. A
6. D
7. B
8. C
9. D
10. A
11. B
12. C
13. A
14. D
15. A
16. D
17. D
18. B
19. C
20. D
21. B
22. A
23. C
24. B
25. A

TEST 6
SYLLABIFICATION

1. B	6. D
2. C	7. D
3. D	8. A
4. A	9. D
5. B	10. B

TEST 7
USAGE

1. D	11. A
2. A	12. D
3. B	13. A
4. D	14. B
5. C	15. B
6. D	16. B
7. C	17. A
8. D	18. B
9. B	19. C
10. D	20. A

21. C
22. B
23. D
24. C
25. B

TEST 8
VOCABULARY

1. adviser
2. pallor
3. waiver
4. squalor
5. defier
6. illimitable
7. aseptic
8. indispensable
9. ignoble
10. imprudent
11. unseasonable
12. immaterial
13. irreducible
14. impalpable
15. unapt, inapt, or inept
16. livable
17. dutiable
18. dirigible
19. accessible
20. forcible
21. p
22. pp.
23. viz.
24. e.g.
25. q.v.
26. machinery
27. missionary
28. promissory
29. distillery
30. provisory
31. mischievous
32. beauteous
33. pretentious
34. scurrilous
35. perspicacious
36. prodigious
37. censorious
38. tumultuous
39. bounteous
40. meritorious
41. abundance
42. coherence
43. beneficence
44. grievance
45. maintenance
46. in the same place; at the same place or in the book already mentioned
47. about; around
48. versus
49. manuscript
50. carbon copy

CLERICAL ABILITIES TEST
EXAMINATION SECTION

DIRECTIONS FOR THIS SECTION:
Each question or incomplete statement is followed by several suggested answers or completions. Select the one that *BEST* answers the question or completes the statement. *PRINT THE LETTER OF THE CORRECT ANSWER IN THE SPACE AT THE RIGHT.*

TEST 1

Questions 1 10.
DIRECTIONS: Questions 1 through 10 consist of lines of names, dates and numbers. For each question, you are to choose the option (A, B, C, or D) in Column II which *EXACTLY* matches the information in Column I. *PRINT THE LETTER OF THE CORRECT ANSWER IN THE SPACE AT THE RIGHT.*

SAMPLE QUESTION

Column I	Column II
Schneider 11/16/75 581932	A. Schneider 11/16/75 518932
	B. Schneider 11/16/75 581932
	C. Schnieder 11/16/75 581932
	D. Shnieder 11/16/75 518932

The correct answer is B. Only option B shows the name, date and number exactly as they are in Column I. Option A has a mistake in the number. Option C has a mistake in the name. Option D has a mistake in the name and in the number.
Now answer Questions 1 through 10 in the same manner.

Column I	Column II	
1. Johnston 12/26/74 659251	A. Johnson 12/23/74 659251	1. ...
	B. Johston 12/26/74 659251	
	C. Johnston 12/26/74 695251	
	D. Johnston 12/26/74 659251	
2. Allison 1/26/75 9939256	A. Allison 1/26/75 9939256	2. ...
	B. Alisson 1/26/75 9939256	
	C. Allison 1/26/76 9399256	
	D. Allison 1/26/75 9993256	
3. Farrell 2/12/75 361251	A. Farell 2/21/75 361251	3. ...
	B. Farrell 2/12/75 361251	
	C. Farrell 2/21/75 361251	
	D. Farrell 2/12/75 361151	
4. Guerrero 4/28/72 105689	A. Guererro 4/28/72 105689	4. ...
	B. Guererro 4/28/72 105986	
	C. Guerrero 4/28/72 105869	
	D. Guerrero 4/28/72 105689	
5. McDonnell 6/05/73 478215	A. McDonnell 6/15/73 478215	5. ...
	B. McDonnell 6/05/73 478215	
	C. McDonnell 6/05/73 472815	
	D. MacDonell 6/05/73 478215	
6. Shepard 3/31/71 075421	A. Sheperd 3/31/71 075421	6. ...
	B. Shepard 3/13/71 075421	
	C. Shepard 3/31/71 075421	
	D. Shepard 3/13/71 075241	
7. Russell 4/01/69 031429	A. Russell 4/01/69 031429	7. ...
	B. Russell 4/10/69 034129	
	C. Russell 4/10/69 031429	
	D. Russell 4/01/69 034129	

8.	Phillips 10/16/68 961042	A.	Philipps	10/16/68	961042	8. ...
		B.	Phillips	10/16/68	960142	
		C.	Phillips	10/16/68	961042	
		D.	Philipps	10/16/68	916042	
9.	Campbell 11/21/72 624856	A.	Campbell	11/21/72	624856	9. ...
		B.	Campbell	11/21/72	624586	
		C.	Campbell	11/21/72	624686	
		D.	Campbel	11/21/72	624856	
10.	Patterson 9/18/71 76199176	A.	Patterson	9/18/72	76191976	10. ...
		B.	Patterson	9/18/71	76199176	
		C.	Patterson	9/18/72	76199176	
		D.	Patterson	9/18/71	76919176	

Questions 11-15.

DIRECTIONS: Questions 11 through 15 consist of groups of numbers and letters which you are to compare. For each question, you are to choose the option (A, B, C, or D) in Column II which *EXACTLY* matches the group of numbers and letters given in Column I.

SAMPLE QUESTION

Column I	Column II
B92466	A. B92644
	B. B94266
	C. A92466
	D. B92466

The correct answer is D. Only option D in Column II shows the group of numbers and letters *EXACTLY* as it appears in Column I.

Now answer Questions 11 through 15 in the same manner.

	Column I	Column II	
11.	925AC5	A. 952CA5	11. ...
		B. 925AC5	
		C. 952AC5	
		D. 925CA6	
12.	Y006925	A. Y060925	12. ...
		B. Y006295	
		C. Y006529	
		D. Y006925	
13.	J236956	A. J236956	13. ...
		B. J326965	
		C. J239656	
		D. J932656	
14.	AB6952	A. AB6952	14. ...
		B. AB9625	
		C. AB9652	
		D. AB6925	
15.	X259361	A. X529361	15. ...
		B. X259631	
		C. X523961	
		D. X259361	

Questions 16-25.

DIRECTIONS: Each of Questions 16 through 25 consists of three lines of code letters and three lines of numbers. The numbers on each line should correspond with the code letters on the same line in accordance with the table below.

Code Letter	S	V	W	A	Q	M	X	E	G	K
Corresponding Number	0	1	2	3	4	5	6	7	8	9

On some of the lines, an error exists in the coding. Compare the letters and numbers in each question carefully. If you find an error or errors on:

only *one* of the lines in the question, mark your answer A;
any *two* lines in the question, mark your answer B;
all *three* lines in the question, mark your answer C;
none of the lines in the question, mark your answer D.

SAMPLE QUESTION

WQGKSXG 2489068
XEKVQMA 6591453
KMAESXV 9527061

In the above example, the first line is correct since each code letter listed has the correct corresponding number. On the second line, an error exists because code letter E should have the number 7 instead of the number 5. On the third line an error exists because the code letter A should have the number 3 instead of the number 2. Since there are errors in two of the three lines, the correct answer is B.
Now answer Questions 16 through 25 in the same manner.

16. SWQEKGA 0247983 16. ...
KEAVSXM 9731065
SSAXGKQ 0036894

17. QAMKMVS 4259510 17. ...
MGGEASX 5897306
KSWMKWS 9125920

18. WKXQWVE 2964217 18. ...
QKXXQVA 4966413
AWMXGVS 3253810

19. GMMKASE 8559307 19. ...
AWVSKSW 3210902
QAVSVGK 4310189

20. XGKQSMK 6894049 20. ...
QSVKEAS 4019730
GSMXKMV 8057951

21. AEKMWSG 3195208 21. ...
MKQSVQK 5940149
XGQAEVW 6843712

22. XGMKAVS 6858310 22. ...
SKMAWEQ 0953174
GVMEQSA 8167403

23. VQSKAVE 1489317 23. ...
WQGKAEM 2489375
MEGKAWQ 5689324

24. XMQVSKG 6541098 24. ...
QMEKEWS 4579720
KMEVKGA 9571983

25. GKVAMEW 8912572 25. ...
AXMVKAE 3651937
KWAGMAV 9238531

Questions 26-35.

DIRECTIONS: Each of Questions 26 through 35 consists of a column of figures. For each question, add the column of figures and choose the correct answer from the four choices given.

26. 5,665.43 26.
2,356.69
6,447.24 A. 20,698.01 B. 21,709.01
7,239.65 C. 21,718.01 D. 22,609.01

27. 817,209.55 27.
264,354.29
82,368.76 A. 1,893,997.49 B. 1,989,988.39
849,964.89 C. 2,009,077.39 D. 2,013,897.49

28. 156,366.89 28.
249,973.23
823,229.49 A. 1,286,439.06 B. 1,287,521.06
56,869.45 C. 1,297,539.06 D. 1,296,421.06

29. 23,422.15 29.
149,696.24
238,377.53
86,289.79 A. 989,229.34 B. 999,879.34
505 544.63 C. 1,003,330.34 D. 1,023,329.34

30. 2,468,926.70 30.
656,842.28
49,723.15 A. 3,218,061.72 B. 3,808,092.72
832,369.59 C. 4,007,861.72 D. 4,818,192.72

31. 524,201.52 31.
7,775,678.51
8,345,299.63
40,628,898.08 A. 88,646,647.81 B. 88,646,747.91
31,374,670.07 C. 88,648,647.91 D. 88,648,747.81

32. 6,824,829.40 32.
682,482.94
5,542,015.27
775,678.51 A. 21,557,513.37 B. 21,567,513.37
7,732,507.25 C. 22,567,503.37 D. 22,567,513.37

33. 22,109,405.58 33.
6 097 093.43
5 050,073.99
8,118,050.05 A. 45,688,593.87 B. 45,688,603.87
4,313,980.82 C. 45,689,593.87 D. 45,689,603.87

34. 79,324,114.19 34.
99,848,129.74
43,331,653.31 A. 264,114,104.38 B. 264,114,114.38
41,610,207.14 C. 265,114,114.38 D. 265,214,104.38

35. 33,729,653.94 35.
5,959,342.58
26,052,715,47
4,452,669.52 A. 76,374,334.10 B. 76,375,334.10
7,079,953.59 C. 77,274,335.10 D. 77,275,335.10

Questions 36-40.

DIRECTIONS: Each of Questions 36 through 40 consists of a single number in Column I and four options in Column II. For each question, you are to choose the option (A, B, C, or D) in Column II which *EXACTLY* matches the number in Column I.

SAMPLE QUESTION

Column I	Column II
5965121	A. 5956121
	B. 5965121
	C. 5966121
	D. 5965211

The correct answer is B. Only option B shows the number *EXACTLY* as it appears in Column I.

Now answer Questions 36 through 40 in the same manner.

	Column I	Column II	
36.	9643242	A. 9643242	36. ...
		B. 9462342	
		C. 9642442	
		D. 9463242	
37.	3572477	A. 3752477	37. ...
		B. 3725477	
		C. 3572477	
		D. 3574277	
38.	5276101	A. 5267101	38. ...
		B. 5726011	
		C. 5271601	
		D. 5276101	
39.	4469329	A. 4496329	39. ...
		B. 4469329	
		C. 4496239	
		D. 4469239	
40.	2326308	A. 2236308	40. ...
		B. 2233608	
		C. 2326308	
		D. 2323608	

TEST 2

Questions 1-5.

DIRECTIONS: Each of Questions 1 through 5 consists of a name and a dollar amount. In each question, the name and dollar amount in Column II should be an exact copy of the name and dollar amount in Column I. If there is:

a mistake only in the name, mark your answer A;
a mistake only in the dollar amount, mark your answer B;
a mistake in both the name and the dollar amount, mark your answer C;
no mistake in either the name or the dollar amount, mark your answer D.

SAMPLE QUESTION

Column I	Column II
George Peterson	George Petersson
$125.50	$125.50

Compare the name and dollar amount in Column II with the name and dollar amount in Column I. The name *Petersson* in Column II is spelle *Peterson* in Column I. The amount is the same in both columns. Sinc there is a mistake only in the name, the answer to the sample question is A.
Now answer Questions 1 through 5 in the same manner.

	Column I	Column II	
1.	Susanne Shultz $3440	Susanne Schultz $3440	1.
2.	Anibal P. Contrucci $2121.61	Anibel P. Contrucci $2112.61	2.
3.	Eugenio Mendoza $12.45	Eugenio Mendozza $12.45	3.
4.	Maurice Gluckstadt $4297	Maurice Gluckstadt $4297	4.
5.	John Pampellonne $4656.94	John Pammpellonne $4566.94	5.

Questions 6-11.

DIRECTIONS: Each of Questions 6 through 11 consists of a set of names and addresses which you are to compare. In each question, t name and addresses in Column II should be an *EXACT* copy of the nam and address in Column I. If there is:

a mistake only in the name, mark your answer A;
a mistake only in the address, mark your answer B;
a mistake in both the name and address, mark your answer C;
no mistake in either the name or address, mark your answer D.

SAMPLE QUESTION

Column I	Column II
Michael Filbert 456 Reade Street New York, N. Y. 10013	Michael Filbert 645 Reade Street New York, N. Y. 10013

Since there is a mistake only in the address (the street number should be 456 instead of 645), the answer to the sample question is B.
Now answer Questions 6 through 11 in the same manner.

	Column I	Column II	
6.	Hilda Goettelmann 55 Lenox Rd. Brooklyn, N. Y. 11226	Hilda Goettelman 55 Lenox Ave. Brooklyn, N. Y. 11226	6.
7.	Arthur Sherman 2522 Batchelder St. Brooklyn, N. Y. 11235	Arthur Sharman 2522 Batcheder St. Brooklyn, N. Y. 11253	7.
8.	Ralph Barnett 300 West 28 Street New York, New York 10001	Ralph Barnett 300 West 28 Street New York, New York 10001	8.
9.	George Goodwin 135 Palmer Avenue Staten Island, New York 10302	George Godwin 135 Palmer Avenue Staten Island, New York 10302	9.
10.	Alonso Ramirez 232 West 79 Street New York, N. Y. 10024	Alonso Ramirez 223 West 79 Street New York, N. Y. 10024	10.
11.	Cynthia Graham 149-35 83 Street Howard Beach, N. Y. 11414	Cynthia Graham 149-35 83 Street Howard Beach, N. Y. 11414	11.

Questions 12-20.

DIRECTIONS: Questions 12 through 20 are problems in subtraction. For each question do the subtraction and select your answer from the four choices given.

12. 232,921.85 A. 52,433.17 B. 52,434.17 12. ...
-179,587.68 C. 53,334.17 D. 53,343.17

13. 5,531,876.29 A. 1,634,717.93 B. 1,644,718.93 13. ...
-3,897,158.36 C. 1,734,717.93 D. 1,734,718.93

14. 1,482,658.22 A. 544,633.46 B. 544,732.46 14. ...
- 937,925.76 C. 545,632.46 D. 545,732.46

15. 937,828.17 A. 678,154.29 B. 679,154.29 15. ...
-259,673.88 C. 688,155.39 D. 699,155.39

16. 760,412.38 A. 496,046.43 B. 496,946.43 16. ...
-263,465.95 C. 496,956.43 D. 497,046.43

17. 3,203,902.26 A. 260,814.30 B. 269,824.30 17. ...
-2,933,087.96 C. 270,814.30 D. 270,824.30

18. 1,023,468.71 A. 88,780.83 B. 88,789.83 18. ...
- 934,678.88 C. 88,880.83 D. 88,889.83

19. 831,549.47 A. 58,734.69 B. 58,834.69 19. ...
-772,814.78 C. 59,735.69 D. 59,834.69

20. 6,306,281.74 A. 2,687,904.99 B. 2,688,904.99 20. ...
-3,617,376.75 C. 2,689,804.99 D. 2,799,905.99

Questions 21-30.

DIRECTIONS: Each of Questions 21 through 30 consists of three lines of code letters and three lines of numbers. The numbers on each line should correspond with the code letters on the same line in accordance with the table below.

Code Letter	J	U	B	T	Y	D	K	R	L	P
Corresponding Number	0	1	2	3	4	5	6	7	8	9

On some of the lines, an error exists in the coding. Compare the letters and numbers in each question carefully. If you find an error or errors on:

only *one* of the lines in the question, mark your answer A;
any *two* lines in the question, mark your answer B;
all *three* lines in the question, mark your answer C;
none of the lines in the question, mark your answer D.

SAMPLE QUESTION

BJRPYUR	2079417
DTBPYKJ	5328460
YKLDBLT	4685283

In the above sample the first line is correct since each code letter listed has the correct corresponding number. On the second line, an error exists because code letter P should have the number 9 instead of the number 8. The third line is correct since each code letter listed has the correct corresponding number. Since there is an error in *one* of the three lines, the correct answer is A.

Now answer Questions 21 through 30 in the same manner.

21.	BYPDTJL	2495308	21. .
	PLRDTJU	9815301	
	DTJRYLK	5207486	
22.	RPBYRJK	7934706	22. .
	PKTYLBU	9624821	
	KDLPJYR	6489047	
23.	TPYBUJR	3942107	23. .
	BYRKPTU	2476931	
	DUKPYDL	5169458	
24.	KBYDLPL	6345898	24. .
	BLRKBRU	2876261	
	JTULDYB	0318542	
25.	LDPYDKR	8594567	25. .
	BDKDRJL	2565708	
	BDRPLUJ	2679810	
26.	PLRLBPU	9858291	26. .
	LPYKRDJ	8936750	
	TDKPDTR	3569527	
27.	RKURPBY	7617924	27. .
	RYUKPTJ	7426930	
	RTKPTJD	7369305	
28.	DYKPBJT	5469203	28. .
	KLPJBTL	6890238	
	TKPLBJP	3698209	
29.	BTPRJYL	2397148	29. .
	LDKUTYR	8561347	
	YDBLRPJ	4528190	
30.	ULPBKYT	1892643	30. .
	KPDTRBJ	6953720	
	YLKJPTB	4860932	

KEYS (CORRECT ANSWERS)

TEST 1

1. D	11. B	21. A	31. D
2. A	12. D	22. C	32. A
3. B	13. A	23. B	33. B
4. D	14. A	24. D	34. A
5. B	15. D	25. A	35. C
6. C	16. D	26. B	36. A
7. A	17. C	27. D	37. C
8. C	18. A	28. A	38. D
9. A	19. D	29. C	39. B
10. B	20. B	30. C	40. C

TEST 2

1. A	11. D	21. B
2. C	12. C	22. C
3. A	13. A	23. D
4. D	14. B	24. B
5. C	15. A	25. A
6. C	16. B	26. C
7. C	17. C	27. A
8. D	18. B	28. D
9. A	19. A	29. B
10. B	20. B	30. D

BASIC FUNDAMENTALS OF FILING SCIENCE

I. COMMENTARY

Filing is the systematic arrangement and storage of papers, cards, forms, catalogues, etc., so that they may be found easily and quickly. The importance of an efficient filing system cannot be emphasized too strongly. The filed materials form records which may be needed quickly to settle questions that may cause embarrassing situations if such evidence is not available. In addition to keeping papers in order so that they are readily available. the filing system must also be designed to keep papers in good condition. A filing system must be planned so that papers may be filed easily, withdrawn easily, and as quickly returned to their proper place. The cost of a filing system is also an important factor.

The need for a filing system arose when the business man began to carry on negotiations on a large scale. He could no longer be intimate with the details of his business. What was needed in the early era was a spindle or pigeon-hole desk. Filing in pigeon-hole desks is now almost completely extinct. It was an unsatisfactory practice since pigeon holes were not labeled, and the desk was an untidy mess.

II. BASIS OF FILING

The science of filing is an exact one and entails a thorough understanding of basic facts, materials, and methods. An overview of this important information now follows.

1. Types of files

(1) SHANNON FILE

This consists of a board, at one end of which are fastened two arches which may be opened laterally.

(2) SPINDLE FILE

This consists of a metal or wood base to which is attached a long, pointed spike. Papers are pushed down on the spike as received. This file is useful for temporary retention of papers.

(3) BOX FILE

This is a heavy cardboard or metal box, opening from the side like a book.

(4) FLAT FILE

This consists of a series of shallow drawers or trays, arranged like drawers in a cabinet.

(5) BELLOWS FILE

This is a heavy cardboard container with alphabetized or compartment sections, the ends of which are closed in such a manner that they resemble an accordion.

(6) VERTICAL FILE

This consists of one or more drawers in which the papers are stood on edge, usually in folders, and are indexed by guides. A series of two or more drawers in one unit is the usual file cabinet.

(7) CLIP FILE

This file has a large clip attached to a board and is very similar to the *SHANNON FILE.*

(8) VISIBLE FILE

Cards are filed flat in an overlapping arrangement which leaves a part of each card visible at all times.

(9) ROTARY FILE

The *ROTARY FILE* has a number of visible card files attached to a post around which they can be revolved. The wheel file has visible cards which rotate around a horizontal axle.

(10) TICKLER FILE

This consists of cards or folders marked with the days of the month, in which materials are filed and turned up on the appropriate day of the month.

2. Aids in filing

(1) GUIDES

Guides are heavy cardboard, pasteboard, or bristolboard sheets the same size as folders. At the top is a tab on which is marked or printed the distinguishing letter, words, or numbers indicating the material filed in a section of the drawer.

(2) SORTING TRAYS

Sorting trays are equipped with alphabetical guides to facilitate the sorting of papers preparatory to placing them in a file.

(3) CODING

Once the classification or indexing caption has been determined, it must be indicated on the letter for filing purposes.

(4) CROSS REFERENCE

Some letters or papers might easily be called for under two or more captions. For this purpose, a cross-reference card or sheet is placed in the folder or in the index.

3. Variations of filing systems

(1) VARIADEX ALPHABETIC INDEX

Provides for more effective expansion of the alphabetic system.

(2) TRIPLE-CHECK NUMERIC FILING

Entails a multiple cross-reference, as the name implies.

(3) VARIADEX FILING

Makes use of color as an aid in filing.

(4) DEWEY DECIMAL SYSTEM

The system is a numeric one used in libraries or for filing library materials in an office. This special type of filing system is used where material is grouped in finely divided categories, such as in libraries. With this method, all material to be filed is divided into ten major groups, from 000 to 900, and then subdivided into tens, units, and decimals.

4. Centralized filing

Centralized filing means keeping the files in one specific or central location. Decentralized filing means putting away papers in files of individual departments. The first step in the organization of a central filing department is to make a careful canvass of all desks in the offices. In this manner we can determine just what material needs to be filed, and what information each desk occupant requires from the central file. Only papers which may be used at some time by persons in the various offices should be placed in the central file. A paper that is to be used at some time by persons in the various offices should be placed in the central file. A paper that is to be used by one department only should never be filed in the central file.

5. Methods of filing

While there are various methods used for filing, actually there are only five basic systems: alphabetical, subject, numerical, geographic, and chronological. All other systems are derived from one of these or from a combination of two or more of them.

Since the purpose of a filing system is to store business records systemically so that any particular record can be found almost instantly when required, filing requires, in addition to the proper kinds of equipment and supplies, an effective method of indexing.

There are five basic systems of filing:

(1) ALPHABETIC FILING

Most filing is alphabetical. Other methods, as described below, require extensive alphabetization.

In alphabetic filing, lettered dividers or guides are arranged in alphabetic sequence. Material to be filed is placed behind the proper guide. All materials under each letter are also arranged alphabetically. Folders are used unless the file is a card index.

(2) SUBJECT FILING

This method is used when a single, complete file on a certain subject is desired. A subject file is often maintained to assemble all correspondence on a certain subject. Such files are valuable in connection with insurance claims, contract negotiations, personnel, and other investigations, special programs, and similar subjects.

(3) GEOGRAPHICAL FILE

Materials are filed according to location: states, cities, counties, or other subdivisions. Statistics and tax information are often filed in this manner.

(4) CHRONOLOGICAL FILE

Records are filed according to date. This method is used especially in "tickler" files that have guides numbered 1 to 31 for each day of the month. Each number indicates the day of the month when the filed item requires attention.

(5) NUMERICAL FILE

This method requires an alphabetic card index giving name and number. The card index is used to locate records numbered consecutively in the files according to date received or sequence in which issued, such as licenses, permits, etc.

6. Indexing

Determining the name or title under which an item is to be filed is known as indexing. For example, how would a letter from Robert E. Smith be filed? The name would be rearranged Smith, Robert E., so that the letter would be filed under the last name.

7. Alphabetizing

The arranging of names for filing is known as alphabetizing. For example, suppose you have four letters indexed under the names Johnson, Becker, Roe, and Stern. How should these letters be arranged in the files so that they may be found easily? You would arrange the four names alphabetically, thus, Becker, Johnson, Roe, and Stern.

III. RULES FOR INDEXING AND ALPHABETIZING

1. The names of persons are to be transposed. Write the surname first, then the given name, and, finally, the middle name or initial. Then arrange the various names according to the alphabetic order of letters throughout the entire name. If there is a title, consider that after the middle name or initial.

NAMES	*INDEXED AS*
Arthur L. Bright	Bright, Arthur L.
Arthur S. Bright	Bright, Arthur S.
P.E. Cole	Cole, P.E.
Dr. John C. Fox	Fox, John C. (Dr.)

2. If a surname includes the same letters of another surname, with one or more additional letters added to the end, the shorter surname is placed first regardless of the given name or the initial of the given name.

NAMES	*INDEXED AS*
Robert E. Brown	Brown, Robert E.
Gerald A. Browne	Browne, Gerald A.
William O. Brownell	Brownell, William O.

3. Firm names are alphabetized under the surnames. Words like the, an, a, of, and for, are not considered.

NAMES	*INDEXED AS*
Bank of America	Bank of America
Bank Discount Dept.	Bank Discount Dept.
The Cranford Press	Cranford Press, The
Nelson Dwyer & Co.	Dwyer, Nelson, & Co.
Sears, Roebuck & Co.	Sears, Roebuck & Co.
Montgomery Ward & Co.	Ward, Montgomery, & Co.

4. The order of filing is determined first of all by the first letter of the names to be filed. If the first letters are the same, the order is determined by the second letters, and so on. In the following pairs of names, the order is determined by the letters underlined:

Austen	Hayes	Hanson	Harvey	Heath	Green	Schwartz
Baker	Heath	Harper	Harwood	Heaton	Greene	Schwarz

5. When surnames are alike, those with initials only precede those with given names, unless the first initial comes alphabetically after the first letter of the name.

Gleason, S.	*but,*	Abbott, Mary
Gleason, S.W.		Abbott, W.B.
Gleason, Sidney		

6. Hyphenated names are treated as if spelled without the hyphen.

Lloyd, Paul N.	Lloyd, Robert
Lloyd-Jones, James	Lloyd-Thomas, A.S.

7. Company names composed of single letters which are not used as abbreviations precede the other names beginning with the same letter.

B & S Garage	E Z Duplicator Co.
B X Cable Co.	Eagle Typewriter Co.
Babbitt, R.N.	Edison Company

8. The ampersand (&) and the apostrophe (') in firm names are disregarded in alphabetizing.

Nelson & Niller	M & C Amusement Corp.
Nelson, Walter J.	M C Art Assn.
Nelson's Bakery	

9. Names beginning with Mac, Mc, or M' are usually placed in regular order as spelled. Some filing systems file separately names beginning with Mc.

MacDonald, R.J.	Mazza, Anthony
Macdonald, S.B.	McAdam, Wm.
Mace, Wm.	McAndrews, Jerry

10. Names beginning with St. are listed as if the name Saint were spelled in full. Numbered street names and all abbreviated names are treated as if spelled out in full.

Saginaw	Fifth Avenue Hotel	Hart Mfg. Co.
St. Louis	42nd Street Dress Shop	Hart, Martin
St. Peter's Rectory	Hart, Chas.	Hart, Thos.
Sandford	Hart, Charlotte	Hart, Thomas A.
Smith, Wm.	Hart, Jas.	Hart, Thos. R.
Smith, Willis	Hart, Janice	

11. Federal, state, or city departments of government should be placed alphabetically under the governmental branch controlling them.
    - Illinois, State of -- Departments and Commissions
        - Banking Dept.
        - Employment Bureau
    - United States Government Departments
        - Commerce
        - Defense
        - State
        - Treasury

12. Alphabetic order

    Each word in a name is an indexing unit. Arrange the names in alphabetic order by comparing similar units in each name. Consider the second units only when the first units are identical. Consider the third units only when both the first and second units are identical.

13. Single surnames or initials

    A surname, when used alone, precedes the same surname with a first name or initial. A surname with a first initial only precedes a surname with a complete first name. This rule is sometimes stated,"nothing comes before something."

14. Surname prefixes

    A surname prefix is not a separate indexing unit, but it is considered part of the surname. These prefixes include: d', D', Da, de, De, Del, Des, Di, Du, Fitz., La, Le, Mc, Mac, 'c, O', St., Van, Van der, Von, Von der, and others. The prefixes M', Mac, and Mc are indexed and filed exactly as they are spelled.

15. Names of firms

    Names of firms and institutions are indexed and filed exactly as they are written when they do not contain the complete name of an individual.

16. Names of firms containing complete individual names

    When the firm or institution name includes the complete name of an individual, the units are transposed for indexing in the same way as the name of an individual.

17. Article "The"

    When the article <u>the</u> occurs at the beginning of a name, it is placed at the end in parentheses but it is not moved. In both cases, it is not an indexing unit and is disregarded in filing.

18. Hyphenated names

    Hyphenated firm names are considered as separate indexing units. Hyphenated surnames of individuals are considered as one indexing unit; this applies also to hyphenated names of individuals whose complete names are part of a firm name.

19. Abbreviations

Abbreviations are considered as though the name were written in full; however, single letters other than abbreviations are considered as separate indexing units.

20. Conjunctions, prepositions and firm endings

Conjunctions and prepositions, such as and, for, in, of, are disregarded in indexing and filing but are not omitted or their order changed when writing names on cards and folders. Firm endings such as Ltd., Inc., Co., Son, Bros., Mfg., and Corp., are treated as a unit in indexing and filing and are considered as though spelled in full, such as Brothers and Incorporated.

21. One or two words

Names that may be spelled either as one or two words are indexed and filed as one word.

22. Compound geographic names

Compound geographic names are considered as separate indexing and filing units, except when the first part of the name is not an English word, such as the Los in Los Angeles.

23. Titles or degrees of individuals, whether preceding or following the name, are not considered in indexing or filing. They are placed in parentheses after the given name or initial. Terms that designate seniority, such as Jr., Sr., 2d, are also placed in parenthese and are considered for indexing and filing only when the names to be indexed are otherwise identical.

<u>Exception A:</u>

When the name of an individual consists of a title and one name only, such as Queen Elizabeth, it is not transposed and the title is considered for indexing and filing.

<u>Exception B:</u>

When a title or foreign article is the initial word of a firm or association name, it is considered for indexing and filing.

24. Possessives

When a word ends in apostrophe s, the s is not considered in indexing and filing. However, when a word ends in s apostrophe, because the s is part of the original word, it is considered. This rule is sometimes stated, "Consider everything up to the apostrophe."

25. United States and foreign government names

Names pertaining to the federal government are indexed and filed under United States Government and then subdivided by title of the department, bureau, division, commission, or board. Names pertaining to foreign governments are indexed and filed under names of countries and then subdivided by title of the department, bureau, division, commission, or board. Phrases, such as department of, bureau of, division of, commission of, board of, when used in titles of governmental bodies, are placed in parentheses after the word they modify, but are disregarded in indexing and filing. Such phrases, however, are considered in indexing and filing nongovernmental names.

26. Other political subdivisions

Names pertaining to other political subdivisions, such as states, counties, cities, or towns, are indexed and filed under the name of the political subdivision and then subdivided by the title of the department, bureau, division, commission, or board.

27. Addresses

When the same name appears with different addresses, the names are indexed as usual and arranged alphabetically according to city or town. The State is considered only when there is duplication of both individual or company name and city name. If the same name is located at different addresses within the same city, then the names are arranged alphabetically by streets. If the same name is located at more than one address on the same street, then the names are arranged from the lower to the higher street number.

28. Numbers

Any number in a name is considered as though it were written in words, and it is indexed and filed as one unit.

29. Bank names

Because the names of many banking institutions are alike in several respects, as first National Bank, Second National Bank, etc., banks are indexed and filed first by city location, then by bank name, with the state location written in parentheses and considered only if necessary

30. Married women

The legal name of a married woman is the one used for filing purposes. Legally, a man's surname is the only part of a man's name a woman assumes when she marries. Her legal name, therefore, could be either:

(1) Her own first and middle names together with her husband's surname, or

(2) Her own first name and maiden surname, together with her husband's surname.

Mrs. is placed in parentheses at the end of the name. Her husband's first and middle names are given in parentheses below her legal name.

31. An alphabetically arranged list of names illustrating many difficult points of alphabetizing follows.

COLUMN I

Abbot , W.B.
Abbott, Alice
Allen, Alexander B.
Allen, Alexander B., Inc.
Andersen, Hans
Andersen, Hans E.
Andersen, Hans E., Jr.
Anderson, Andrew
Andrews, George
Brown Motor Co., Boston
Brown Motor Co., Chicago
Brown Motor Co., Philadelphia
Brown Motor Co., San Francisco
Dean, Anna
Dean, Anna F.
Dean, Anna Frances
Dean & Co.
Deane-Arnold Apartments
Deane's Pharmacy
Deans, Felix A.
Dean's Studio
Deans, Wm.
Deans & Williams
East Randolph
East St.Louis
Easton, Pa.
Eastport, Me.

COLUMN II

54th St. Tailor Shop
Forstall, W.J.
44th St. Garage
M A Delivery Co.
M & C Amusement Corp.
M C Art Assn.
MacAdam, Wm.
Macaulay, James
MacAulay, Wilson
MacDonald, R.J.
Macdonald, S.B.
Mace, Wm.
MacMahon, L.S.
Madison, Seth
Mazza, Anthony
McAdam, Wm.
McAndrews, Jerry
Meade & Clark Co.
Meade, S.T.
Meade, Solomon
Sackett Publishing Co.
Sacks, Robert
St.Andrew Hotel
St.John,Homer W.
Saks,Isaac B.
Stephens,Ira
Stevens,Delevan
Stevens,Delila

IV. OFFICIAL EXAMINATION DIRECTIONS AND RULES

To preclude the possibility of conflicting or varying methods of filing, explicit directions and express rules are given to the candidate before he answers the filing questions on an examination.

The most recent official directions and rules for the filing questions are given immediately hereafter.

OFFICIAL DIRECTIONS

Each of questions ... to ... consists of four(five)names. For each question, select the one of the four(five)names that should be first (second)(third)(last) if the four(five)names were arranged in alphabetical order in accordance with the rules for alphabetical filing given below. Read these rules carefully. Then, for each question, indicate in the correspondingly numbered row on the answer sheet the letter preceding the name that should be first(second)(third)(last) in alphabetical order.

OFFICIAL RULES FOR ALPHABETICAL FILING

Names of Individuals

1. The names of individuals are filed in strict alphabetical order, first according to the last name, then according to first name or initial, and, finally, according to middle name or initial. For example: William Jones precedes George Kirk and Arthur S. Blake precedes Charles M. Blake.
2. When the last names are identical, the one with an initial instead of a first name precedes the one with a first name beginning with the same initial. For example: J.Green precedes Joseph Green.
3. When identical last names also have identical first names, the one without a middle name or initial precedes the one with a middle name or initial. For example: Robert Jackson precedes both Robert C.Jackson and Robert Chester Jackson.
4. When last names are identical and the first names are also identical, the one with a middle initial precedes the one with a middle name beginning with the same initial. For example: Peter A. Brown precedes Peter Alvin Brown.
5. Prefixes such as De, El, La, and Van are considered parts of the names they precede. For example: Wilfred DeWald precedes Alexander Duval.
6. Last names beginning with "Mac" or "Mc" are filed as spelled.
7. Abbreviated names are treated as if they were spelled out. For example: Jos. is filed as Joseph and Robt. is filed as Robert.
8. Titles and designations such as Dr., Mrs., Prof. are disregarded in filing.

Names of Business Organizations

1. The names of business organizations are filed exactly as written, except that an organization bearing the name of an individual is filed alphabetically according to the name of the individual in accordance with the rules for filing names of individuals given above. For example: Thomas Allison Machine Company precedes Northern Baking Company.
2. When numerals occur in a name, they are treated as if they were spelled out. For example: 6 stands for six and 4th stands for fourth.
3. When the following words occur in names, they are disregarded: the, of, and. Sample: Choose the name that should be filed *third*.

(A) Fred Town (2)	(C) D. Town (1)
(B) Jack Towne (3)	(D) Jack S.Towne (4)

The numbers in parentheses indicate the proper alphabetical order in which these names should be filed. Since the name that should be filed third is Jack Towne, the answer is (B).

FILING
EXAMINATION SECTION

TEST 1

DIRECTIONS FOR THIS SECTION: Each of the following questions contains four names. For each question, choose the name that should be *FIRST* if the four names are to be arranged in alphabetical order in accordance with the Rules for Alphabetical Filing given before. Read these rules carefully. Then, for each question, indicate in the space at the right the letter before the name that should be *FIRST* in alphabetical order.

SAMPLE QUESTION

A. Jane Earl (2)
B. James A. Earle (4)
C. James Earl (1)
D. J. Earle (3)

The numbers in parentheses show the proper alphabetical order in which these names should be filed. Since the name that should be filed *FIRST* is James Earl, the answer to the Sample Question is C.

1. A. Majorca Leather Goods
B. Robert Maiorca and Sons
C. Maintenance Management Corp.
D. Majestic Carpet Mills
1. ...

2. A. Municipal Telephone Service
B. Municipal Reference Library
C. Municipal Credit Union
D. Municipal Broadcasting System
2. ...

3. A. Robert B. Pierce B. R. Bruce Pierce
C. Ronald Pierce D. Robert Bruce Pierce
3. ...

4. A. Four Seasons Sports Club
B. 14 Street Shopping Center
C. Forty Thieves Restaurant
D. 42nd St. Theaters
4. ...

5. A. Franco Franceschini B. Amos Franchini
C. Sandra Franceschia D. Lilie Franchinesca
5. ...

TEST 2

DIRECTIONS FOR THIS SECTION: Same as for Test 1.

1. A. Alan Carson, M. D.
B. The Andrew Carlton Nursing Home
C. Prof. Alfred P. Carlton
D. Mr. A. Peter Carlton
1. ...

2. A. Chas. A. Denner B. H. Jeffrey Dener
C. Charles Denner D. Harold Dener
2. ...

3. A. James C. Maziola B. Joseph A. Mazzola
C. James Maziola D. J. Alfred Mazzola
3. ...

4. A. Bureau of Family Affairs
B. Office of the Comptroller
C. Department of Gas & Electricity
D. Board of Estimate
4. ...

5. A. Robert Alan Pearson B. John Charles Pierson 5. ...
C. Robert Allen Pearson D. John Chester Pierson

6. A. The Johnson Manufacturing Co. 6. ...
B. C. J. Johnston
C. Bernard Johnsen
D. Prof. Corey Johnstone

7. A. Ninteenth Century Book Shop 7. ...
B. Ninth Federal Bank
C. 19th Hole Coffee Shop
D. 92nd St. Station

8. A. George S. McNeely B. Hugh J. MacIntosh 8. ...
C. Mr. G. Stephen McNeally D. Mr. H. James MacIntosh

TEST 3

DIRECTIONS FOR THIS SECTION: Each of the following questions consists of four names. For each question, choose the one of the four names that should be *LAST* if the four names were arranged in alphabetical order in accordance with the Rules for Alphabetical Filing given before. Read these rules carefully. Then, for each question, indicate in the space at the right the letter before the name that should be *LAST* in alphabetical order.

SAMPLE QUESTION

A. Jane Earl (2)
B. James A. Earle (4)
C. James Earl (1)
D. J. Earle (3)

The numbers in parentheses show the proper alphabetical order in which these names should be filed. Since the name that should be filed *LAST* is James A. Earle, the answer to the Sample Question is B.

1. A. Steiner,Michael B. Steinblau, Dr. Walter 1. ...
C. Steinet, Gary D. Stein, Prof. Edward

2. A. The Paper Goods Warehouse 2. ...
B. T. Pane and Sons Inc.
C. Paley, Wallace
D. Painting Supplies Inc.

3. A. D'Angelo, F. B. De Nove, C. 3. ...
C. Daniels, Frank D. Dovarre, Carl

4. A. Berene, Arnold B. Berene, Arnold L. 4. ...
C. Beren, Arnold Lee D. Berene, A.

5. A. Kallinski, Liza B. Kalinsky, L. 5. ...
C. Kallinky, E. D. Kallinsky, Elizabeth

6. A. Morgeno, Salvatore 6. ...
B. Megan, J.
C. J. Morgenthal Consultant Services
D. Morgan, Janet

7. A. Ritter, G. B. Ritter, George 7. ...
C. Riter, George H. D. Ritter, G. H.

8. A. Wheeler, Adele N. B. Wieler, Ada 8. ...
C. Weiler, Adelaide D. Wheiler, Adele

9. A. Macan, Toby B. Maccini, T. 9. ...
C. MacAvoy, Thomas D. Mackel, Theodore

10. A. Loomus, Kenneth 10. ...
B. Lomis Paper Supplies
C. Loo, N.
D. Loomis Machine Repair Company

TEST 4

DIRECTIONS FOR THIS SECTION: In the following questions,there are five notations numbered 1 through 5 shown in Column I. Each notation is made up of a supplier's name, a contract number, and a date and is to be filed according to the following rules:

First: File in alphabetical order.
Second: When two or more notations have the same supplier, file according to the contract number in numerical order beginning with the lowest number.
Third: When two or more notations have the same supplier and contract number, file according to the date beginning with the earliest date.

In Column II the numbers 1 through 5 are arranged in four ways to show different possible orders in which the merchandise information might be filed. Pick the answer (A, B, C, or D) in Column II in which the notations are arranged according to the above filing rules.

SAMPLE QUESTION

Column I	Column II
1. Cluney (4865) 6/17/72	A. 2, 3, 4, 1, 5
2. Roster (2466) 5/10/71	B. 2, 5, 1, 3, 4
3. Altool (7114) 10/15/72	C. 3, 2, 1, 4, 5
4. Cluney (5276) 12/18/71	D. 3, 5, 1, 4, 2
5. Cluney (4865) 4/8/72	

The *correct* way to file the notations is:
3. Altool (7114) 10/15/72
5. Cluney (4865) 4/8/72
1. Cluney (4865) 6/17/72
4. Cluney (5276) 12/18/71
2. Roster (2466) 5/10/71

The correct filing order is shown by the numbers in front of each name (3, 5, 1, 4, 2). The answer to the Sample Question is the letter in Column II in front of the numbers 3, 5, 1, 4, 2. This answer is D.

	Column I	Column II	
1.	1. Fenten (38511) 1/4/73	A. 3, 5, 2, 1, 4	1. ...
	2. Meadowlane (5020) 11/1/72	B. 4, 1, 2, 5, 3	
	3. Whitehall (36142) 6/22/72	C. 4, 2, 5, 3, 1	
	4. Clinton (4141) 5/26/71	D. 5, 4, 3, 1, 2	
	5. Mester (8006) 4/20/71		

	Column I	Column II	
2.	1. Harvard (2286) 2/19/70	A. 2, 4, 3, 1, 5	2. ...
	2. Parker (1781) 4/12/72	B. 2, 1, 3, 4, 5	
	3. Lenson (9044) 6/6/72	C. 4, 1, 3, 2, 5	
	4. Brothers (38380) 10/11/72	D. 5, 2, 3, 1, 4	
	5. Parker (41400) 12/20/70		
3.	1. Newtone (3197) 8/22/70	A. 1, 4, 2, 5, 3	3. ...
	2. Merritt (4071) 8/8/72	B. 4, 2, 1, 5, 3	
	3. Writebest (60666) 4/7/71	C. 4, 5, 2, 1, 3	
	4. Maltons (34380) 3/30/72	D. 5, 2, 4, 3, 1	
	5. Merrit (4071) 7/16/71		
4.	1. Weinburt (45514) 6/4/71	A. 4, 5, 2, 1, 3	4. ...
	2. Owntye (35860) 10/4/72	B. 4, 2, 5, 3, 1	
	3. Weinburt (45514) 2/1/72	C. 4, 2, 5, 1, 3	
	4. Fasttex (7677) 11/10/71	D. 4, 5, 2, 3, 1	
	5. Owntye (4574) 7/17/72		
5.	1. Premier (1003) 7/29/70	A. 2, 1, 4, 3, 5	5. ...
	2. Phylson (0031) 5/5/72	B. 3, 5, 4, 1, 2	
	3. Lathen (3328) 10/3/71	C. 4, 1, 2, 3, 5	
	4. Harper (8046) 8/18/72	D. 4, 3, 5, 2, 1	
	5. Lathen (3328) 12/1/72		
6.	1. Repper (46071) 10/14/72	A. 3, 2, 4, 5, 1	6. ...
	2. Destex (77271) 8/27/72	B. 3, 4, 2, 5, 1	
	3. Clawson (30736) 7/28/71	C. 3, 4, 5, 2, 1	
	4. Destex (27207) 8/17/71	D. 3, 5, 4, 2, 1	
	5. Destex (77271) 4/14/71		

TEST 5

DIRECTIONS FOR THIS SECTION: Each of the following questions represents five cards to be filed, numbered 1 through 5 shown in Column I. Each card is made up of the employee's name, a work assignment code number shown in parentheses, and the date of this assignment. The cards are to be filed according to the following rules:

First: File in alphabetical order.

Second: When two or more cards have the same employee's name, file according to the work assignment number beginning with the lowest number.

Third: When two or more cards have the same employee's name and same assignment number, file according to the assignment date beginning with the earliest date.

Column II shows the cards arranged in four different orders. Pick the answer (A, B, C, or D) in Column II which shows the cards arranged correctly according to the above filing rules.

SAMPLE QUESTION: See Sample Question (with answer) for Test 4.

Now answer the following questions according to these rules.

	Column I			Column II	
1.	1. Prichard	(013469)	4/6/71	A. 5, 4, 3, 2, 1	1. ...
	2. Parks	(678941)	2/7/71	B. 1, 2, 5, 3, 4	
	3. Williams	(551467)	3/6/70	C. 2, 1, 5, 3, 4	
	4. Wilson	(551466)	8/9/67	D. 1, 5, 4, 3, 2	
	5. Stanhope	(300014)	8/9/67		
2.	1. Ridgeway	(623809)	8/11/71	A. 5, 1, 3, 4, 2	2. ...
	2. Travers	(305439)	4/5/67	B. 5, 1, 3, 2, 4	
	3. Tayler	(818134)	7/5/68	C. 1, 5, 3, 2, 4	
	4. Travers	(305349)	5/6/70	D. 1, 5, 4, 2, 3	
	5. Ridgeway	(623089)	10/9/71		
3.	1. Jaffe	(384737)	2/19/71	A. 3, 5, 2, 4, 1	3. ...
	2. Inez	(859176)	8/8/72	B. 3, 5, 2, 1, 4	
	3. Ingrahm	(946460)	8/6/69	C. 2, 3, 5, 1, 4	
	4. Karp	(256146)	5/5/70	D. 2, 3, 5, 4, 1	
	5. Ingrahm	(946460)	6/4/70		
4.	1. Marrano	(369421)	7/24/69	A. 1, 5, 3, 4, 2	4. ...
	2. Marks	(652910)	2/23/71	B. 3, 5, 4, 2, 1	
	3. Netto	(556772)	3/10/72	C. 2, 4, 1, 5, 3	
	4. Marks	(652901)	2/17/72	D. 4, 2, 1, 5, 3	
	5. Netto	(556772)	6/17/70		
5.	1. Abernathy	(712467)	6/23/70	A. 5, 3, 1, 2, 4	5. ...
	2. Acevedo	(680262)	6/23/68	B. 5, 4, 2, 3, 1	
	3. Aaron	(967647)	1/17/69	C. 1, 3, 5, 2, 4	
	4. Acevedo	(680622)	5/14/67	D. 2, 4, 1, 5, 3	
	5. Aaron	(967647)	4/1/65		
6.	1. Simon	(645219)	8/19/70	A. 4, 1, 2, 5, 3	6. ...
	2. Simon	(645219)	9/2/68	B. 4, 5, 2, 1, 3	
	3. Simons	(645218)	7/7/70	C. 3, 5, 2, 1, 4	
	4. Simms	(646439)	10/12/71	D. 5, 1, 2, 3, 4	
	5. Simon	(645219)	10/16/67		
7.	1. Rappaport	(312230)	6/11/71	A. 4, 3, 1, 2, 5	7. ...
	2. Rascio	(777510)	2/9/70	B. 4, 3, 1, 5, 2	
	3. Rappaport	(312230)	7/3/67	C. 3, 4, 1, 5, 2	
	4. Rapaport	(312330)	9/6/70	D. 5, 2, 4, 3, 1	
	5. Rascio	(777501)	7/7/70		
8.	1. Johnson	(843250)	6/8/67	A. 1, 3, 2, 4, 5	8. ...
	2. Johnson	(843205)	4/3/70	B. 1, 3, 2, 5, 4	
	3. Johnson	(843205)	8/6/67	C. 3, 2, 1, 4, 5	
	4. Johnson	(843602)	3/8/71	D. 3, 2, 1, 5, 4	
	5. Johnson	(843602)	8/3/70		

TEST 6

DIRECTIONS FOR THIS SECTION: In each of the following questions there are four groups of names. One of the groups in each question is *NOT* in correct alphabetic order. Mark the letter of that group next to the number that corresponds to the number of the question.

1. A. Ace Advertising Agency; Acel, Erwin; Ad Graphics; Ade, E. J. & Co. 1. ...
   B. Advertising Bureau, Inc.; Advertising Guild, Inc.; Advertising Ideas, Inc.; Advertising Sales Co.
   C. Allan Associates; Allen-Wayne, Inc.; Alley & Richards, Inc.; Allum, Ralph
   D. Anderson & Cairnes; Amos Parrish & Co.; Anderson Merrill Co.; Anderson, Milton
2. A. Bach, Henry; Badillo, John; Baer, Budd; Bair, Albert 2. ...
   B. Baker, Lynn; Bakers, Albert; Bailin, Henry; Bakers Franchise Corp.
   C. Bernhardt, Manfred; Bernstein, Jerome; Best, Frank; Benton Associates
   D. Brandford, Edward; Branstatter Associates; Brown, Martel; Browne, Bert
3. A. Cone, Robert; Contempo, Bernard; Conti Advertising; Cooper, James 3. ...
   B. Cramer, Zed; Creative Sales; Crofton, Ada; Cromwell, Samuel
   C. Cheever, Fred; Chernow Advertising; Chenault Associates; Chesler, Arthur
   D. Chain Store Advertising; Chair Lawrence & Co.; Chaite, Alexander E.; Chase, Luis
4. A. Delahanty, Francis; Dela McCarthy Associates; Delehanty, Kurnit; Delroy, Stewart 4. ...
   B. Doerfler, B. R.; Doherty, Clifford; Dorchester Apartments; Dorchester, Monroe
   C. Drayer, Stella; Dreher, Norton; Dreyer, Harvey; Dryer, Lester
   D. Duble, Normal; Duevell, William C.; Du Fine, August; Dugan, Harold
5. A. Esmond, Walter; Esty, Willia; Ettinger, Carl; Everett, Austin 5. ...
   B. Enlos, Cartez; Entertainment, Inc.; Englemore, Irwin; Equity Associates
   C. Einhorn, Anna Mrs.; Einhorn, Arlene; Eisele, Mary; Eisele, Minnie Mrs.
   D. Eagen, Roy; Egale, George; Egan, Barrett; Eisen, Henry
6. A. Funt-Rand Inc.; Furman, Fainer & Co.; Furman Roth & Co.; Fusco, Frank A. 6. ...
   B. Friedan, Phillip; Friedman, Mitchell; Friend, Harvey; Friend, Herbert
   C. Folkart Greeting Cards; Food Service; Foote, Cornelius; Foreign Advertising
   D. Finkels, Eliot; Finnerman, John; Finneran, Joseph; Firestone, Albert
7. A. Gubitz, Jay; Guild, Dorothy; Gumbiner, B.; Gussow, Leonard 7. ...
   B. Gore, Smith; Gotham Art, Inc.; Gotham Editors Service; Gotham-Vladimir, Inc.
   C. Georgian, Wolf; Gerdts, H. J.; German News Co.; Germaine, Werner
   D. Gardner, Fred; Gardner, Roy; Garner, Roy; Gaynor & Ducal, Inc.

8\. A. Howard, E. T.; Howard, Francis; Howson, Allen; Hoyt, Charles 8. ...
B. Houston, Byron; House of Graphics; Howland, Lynne; Hoyle, Mortimer
C. Hi-Lite Art Service; Hickerson, J. M.; Hickey, Murphy; Hicks, Gilbert
D. Hyman, Bram; Hyman, Charles B.; Hyman, Claire; Hyman, Claude

9\. A. Idone, Leopold; Ingraham, Evelyn; Ianuzzi, Frank; Itkin, Simon 9. ...
B. Ideas, Inc.; Inter-Racial Press, Inc.; International Association; Iverson, Ford
C. Il Trionofo; Inwood Bake Shop; Iridor, Rose; Italian Pastry
D. Ionadi, Anthony; Irena, Louise; Iris, Ysabella; Isabelle, Arlia

10\. A. Jonas, Myron; Johnstone, John; Jones, Julius; Joptha, Meyer 10. ...
B. Jeanne's Beauty Shoppe; Jeger, Jans; Jem, H.; Jim's Grill
C. Jacobs, Abraham & Co.; Jacobs, Harold A.; Jacobs, Joseph; Jacobs, M. J.
D. Japan Air Lines; Jensen, Arne; Judson, P.; Juliano, Jeremiah

TEST 7

DIRECTIONS FOR THIS SECTION: Below are ten groups of names, numbered 1 through 10. For each group, three different filing arrangements of the names in the group are given. In only *ONE* of these arrangements are the names in correct filing order according to standard rules for filing. For each group, select the *ONE* arrangement, lettered A, B, C, that is *CORRECT*.

1\. 1. ...

Arrangement A
Nichols, C. Arnold
Nichols, Bruce
Nicholson, Arthur

Arrangement B
Nichols, Bruce
Nichols, C. Arnold
Nicholson, Arthur

Arrangement C
Nicholson, Arthur
Nichols, Bruce
Nichols, C. Arnold

2\. 2. ...

Arrangement A
Schaefer's Drug Store
Schaefer, Harry T.
Schaefer Bros.

Arrangement B
Schaefer Bros.
Schaefer, Harry T.
Schaefer's Drug Store

Arrangement C
Schaefer Bros.
Schaefer's Drug Store
Schaefer, Harry T.

3\. 3. ...

Arrangement A
Adams' Dime Store
Adami, David
Adams, Donald

Arrangement B
Adami, David
Adams' Dime Store
Adams, Donald

Arrangement C
Adami, David
Adams, Donald
Adams' Dime Store

4. *Arrangement A*
Newton, Jas. F.
Newton, Janet
Newton-Jarvis Law Firm

Arrangement B
Newton-Jarvis Law Firm
Newton, Jas. F.
Newton, Janet

Arrangement C
Newton, Janet
Newton-Jarvis Law Firm
Newton, Jas. F.

4. ...

5. *Arrangement A*
Radford and Bigelow
Radford Transfer Co.
Radford-Smith, Albert

Arrangement B
Radford and Bigelow
Radford-Smith, Albert
Radford Transfer Co.

Arrangement C
Radford Transfer Co.
Radford and Bigelow
Radford-Smith, Albert

5. ...

6. *Arrangement A*
Trent, Inc.
Trent Farm Products
20th Century Film Corp.

Arrangement B
20th Century Film Corp.
Trent Farm Products
Trent, Inc.

Arrangement C
Trent Farm Products
Trent, Inc.
20th Century Film Corp.

6. ...

7. *Arrangement A*
Morrell, Ralph
M.R.B. Paper Co.
Mt.Ranier Hospital

Arrangement B
Morrell, Ralph
Mt.Ranier Hospital
M.R.B. Paper Co.

Arrangement C
M.R.B. Paper Co.
Morrell, Ralph
Mt.Ranier Hospital

7. ...

8. *Arrangement A*
Vanity Faire Shop
Van Loon, Charles
The Williams Magazine Corp.

Arrangement B
The Williams Magazine Corp.
Van Loon, Charles
Vanity Faire Shop

Arrangement C
Van Loon, Charles
Vanity Faire Shop
The Williams Magazine Corp.

8. ...

9. *Arrangement A*
Crane and Jones Ins. Co.
Little Folks Shop
L. J. Coughtry Mfg. Co.

Arrangement B
L. J. Coughtry Mfg. Co.
Crane and Jones Ins. Co.
Little Folks Shop

Arrangement C
Little Folks Shop
L. J. Coughtry Mfg. Co.
Crane and Jones Ins. Co.

9. ...

10. *Arrangement A*
South Arlington Garage
N. Y. State Dept. of
Audit and Control
State Antique Shop

Arrangement B
N. Y. State Dept. of
Audit and Control
South Arlington Garage
State Antique Shop

Arrangement C
State Antique Shop
South Arlington Garage
N. Y. State Dept. of
Audit and Control

10. ...

TEST 8

DIRECTIONS FOR THIS SECTION: Same as for Test 7.

	Arrangement A	Arrangement B	Arrangement C	
1.	Gillilan,William Gililane, Ethel Gillihane,Harry	Gililane, Ethel Gillihane,Harry Gillilan,William	Gillihane, Harry Gillilan, William Gililane, Ethel	1. ...
2.	Stevens,J.Donald Stevenson, David Stevens, James	Stevenson, David Stevens,J.Donald Stevens, James	Stevens,J.Donald Stevens, James Stevenson, David	2. ...
3.	Brooks, Arthur E. Brooks,H.Albert Brooks, H.T.	Brooks, H.T. Brooks,H.Albert Brooks,Arthur E.	Brooks,H.Albert Brooks, Arthur E. Brooks, H.T.	3. ...
4.	Lafayette, Earl Le Grange, Wm. J. La Roux Haberdashery	Le Grange, Wm. J. La Roux Haberdashery Lafayette, Earl	Lafayette, Earl La Roux Haberdashery Le Grange, Wm. J.	4. ...
5.	Mosher Bros. Mosher's Auto Repair Mosher, Dorothy	Mosher's Auto Repair Mosher Bros. Mosher, Dorothy	Mosher Bros. Mosher, Dorothy Mosher's Auto Repair	5. ...
6.	Ainsworth, Inc. Ainsworth,George Air-O-Pad Co.	Ainsworth, George Ainsworth, Inc. Air-O-Pad Co.	Air-O-Pad Co. Ainsworth, George Ainsworth, Inc.	6. ...
7.	Peters' Printing Co. Peterbridge, Alfred Peters, Paul	Peterbridge, Alfred Peters, Paul Peters' Printing Co.	Peters, Paul Peters' Printing Co. Peterbridge, Alfred	7. ...
8.	Sprague-Miller, Ella Sprague (and) Reed Sprague Insurance Co.	Sprague (and) Reed Sprague Insurance Co. Sprague-Miller, Ella	Sprague Insurance Co. Sprague (and) Reed Sprague-Miller, Ella	8. ...
9.	Ellis, Chalmers Adv. Agency Ellis, Chas. Ellis, Charlotte	Ellis, Chas. Ellis, Charlotte Ellis, Chalmers Adv. Agency		9. ...

Arrangement C
Ellis, Charlotte
Ellis, Chas.
Ellis, Chalmers Adv. Agency

10. *Arrangement A*
Adams, Paul
Five Acres Coffee Shop
Fielding Adjust. Co.

Arrangement B
Five Acres Coffee Shop
Adams, Paul
Fielding Adjust. Co.

Arrangement C
Adams, Paul
Fielding Adjust. Co.
Five Acres Coffee Chop

10. ...

TEST 9

DIRECTIONS FOR THIS SECTION: Below in Section A is a diagram representing 40 divisional drawers in alphabetic file, numbered 1 through 40. Below in Section B is a list of 30 names to be filed, numbered 1 through 30, with a drawer number opposite each name, representing the drawer in which it is assumed a file clerk has filed the name.

Determine which are filed *CORRECTLY* and which are filed *INCORRECTLY* based on standard rules for indexing and filing. If the name is filed *CORRECTLY*, print in the space at the right the letter C. If the name is filed *INCORRECTLY*, print in the space at the right the letter I.

SECTION A

1 Aa-Al	6 Bs-Bz	11 Ea-Er	16 Gp-Gz	21 Kp-Kz	26 Mo-Mz	31 Qa-Qz	36 Ta-Ti
2 Am-Au	7 Ca-Ch	12 Es-Ez	17 Ha-Hz	22 La-Le	27 Na-Nz	32 Ra-Rz	37 Tj-Tz
3 Av-Az	8 Ci-Co	13 Fa-Fr	18 Ia-Iz	23 Lf-Lz	28 Oa-Oz	33 Sa-Si	38 U-V
4 Ba-Bi	9 Cp-Cz	14 Fa-Fz	19 Ja-Jz	24 Ma-Mi	29 Pa-Pr	34 Sj-St	39 Wa-Wz
5 Bj-Br	10 Da-Dz	15 Ga-Go	20 Ka-Ko	25 Mj-Mo	30 Ps-Pz	35 Su-Sz	40 X-Y-Z

SECTION B

	Name or Title	Drawer No.	
1.	William O'Dea	28	1. ...
2.	J. Arthur Crawford	8	2. ...
3.	DuPont Chemical Co.	10	3. ...
4.	Arnold Bros. Mfg. Co.	2	4. ...
5.	Dr. Charles Ellis	10	5. ...
6.	Gray and Doyle Adv. Agency	16	6. ...

Name or Title	Drawer No.	
7. Tom's Smoke Shop	37	7. ...
8. Wm. E. Jarrett Motor Corp.	39	8. ...
9. Penn-York Air Service	29	9. ...
10. Corinne La Fleur	13	10. ...
11. Cartright, Incorporated	7	11. ...
12. 7th Ave. Market	24	12. ...
13. Ft. Schuyler Apts.	13	13. ...
14. Madame Louise	23	14. ...
15. Commerce Dept., U. S. Govt.	38	15. ...
16. Norman Bulwer-Lytton	6	16. ...
17. Hilton Memorial Library	17	17. ...
18. The Linen Chest Gift Shop	36	18. ...
19. Ready Mix Supply Co.	32	19. ...
20. City Service Taxi	8	20. ...
21. A.R.C. Transportation Co.	37	21. ...
22. New Jersey Insurance Co.	19	22. ...
23. Capt. Larry Keith	20	23. ...
24. Girl Scouts Council	15	24. ...
25. University of Michigan	24	25. ...
26. Sister Ursula	38	26. ...
27. Am. Legion Post #9	22	27. ...
28. Board of Hudson River Reg. Dist.	17	28. ...
29. Mid West Bus Lines	39	29. ...
30. South West Tours, Inc.	34	30. ...

TEST 10

DIRECTIONS FOR THIS SECTION: Each question or incomplete statement is followed by several suggested answers or completions. Select the one that BEST answers the question or completes the statement. *PRINT THE LETTER OF THE CORRECT ANSWER IN THE SPACE AT THE RIGHT.*

1. Of the following statements about the numeric system of filing, the one which is CORRECT is that it — 1. ...
   A. is the least accurate of all methods of filing
   B. eliminates the need for cross-referencing
   C. allows for very limited expansion
   D. requires a separate index
2. When more than one name or subject is involved in a piece of correspondence to be filed, the office assistant should, *generally*, — 2. ...
   A. prepare a cross-reference sheet
   B. establish a geographical filing system
   C. prepare out-guides
   D. establish a separate index card file for noting such correspondence
3. A tickler file is MOST generally used for — 3. ...
   A. identification of material contained in a numeric file
   B. maintenance of a current listing of telephone numbers
   C. follow-up of matters requiring future attention
   D. control of records borrowed or otherwise removed from the file

4. In filing, the name Ms. "Ann Catalana-Moss" should *generally* be indexed as 4. ...
   A. Moss, Catalana, Ann (Ms.)
   B. Catalana-Moss, Ann (Ms.)
   C. Ann Catalana-Moss (Ms.)
   D. Moss-Catalana, Ann (Ms.)
5. An office assistant has a set of four cards, each of which contains one of the following names. In alphabetic filing, the FIRST of the cards to be filed is 5. ...
   A. (Ms.) Alma John
   B. Mrs. John (Patricia) Edwards
   C. John-Edward School Supplies, Inc.
   D. John H. Edwards
6. *Generally*, of the following, the name to be filed FIRST in an alphabetical filing system is 6. ...
   A. Diane Maestro
   B. Diana McElroy
   C. James Mackell
   D. James McKell
7. According to *generally* recognized rules of filing in an alphabetic filing system, the one of the following names which normally should be filed LAST is 7. ...
   A. Department of Education, New York State
   B. F. B. I.
   C. Police Department of New York City
   D. P. S. 81 of New York City

KEYS (CORRECT ANSWERS)

TEST 1	
1.	C
2.	D
3.	B
4.	D
5.	C

TEST 2	
1.	D
2.	B
3.	C
4.	B
5.	A
6.	C
7.	A
8.	D

TEST 3	
1.	C
2.	A
3.	D
4.	B
5.	D
6.	C
7.	B
8.	B
9.	D
10.	A

TEST 4	
1.	B
2.	C
3.	C
4.	A
5.	D
6.	C

TEST 5	
1.	C
2.	A
3.	C
4.	D
5.	A
6.	B
7.	B
8.	D

TEST 6	
1.	D
2.	B
3.	C
4.	A
5.	B
6.	D
7.	C
8.	B
9.	A
10.	A

TEST 7	
1.	B
2.	C
3.	B
4.	A
5.	B
6.	C
7.	A
8.	A
9.	B
10.	B

TEST 8	
1.	B
2.	C
3.	A
4.	C
5.	B
6.	B
7.	B
8.	C
9.	A
10.	C

TEST 9			
1.	C	16.	C
2.	I	17.	C
3.	C	18.	I
4.	C	19.	C
5.	I	20.	C
6.	C	21.	I
7.	C	22.	I
8.	I	23.	C
9.	C	24.	C
10.	I	25.	I
11.	C	26.	I
12.	I	27.	I
13.	C	28.	C
14.	I	29.	I
15.	C	30.	C

TEST 10	
1.	D
2.	A
3.	C
4.	B
5.	D
6.	C
7.	B

The Typing Test

In the test of ability to type, the applicant meets a single task, that of copying material exactly as it is presented. He must demonstrate how rapidly he can do so and with what accuracy. A specimen of the typing test is shown as Exhibit No. 6.

How the Test Is Given

In order to follow usual examination procedure in giving the test, each competitor will need a copy of the test and two sheets of typewriter paper. About 15 minutes will be needed for the complete typing test.

Three minutes are allowed for reading the instructions on the face of the test and 3 minutes for the practice typing. The practice exercise consists of typing instructions as to spacing, capitalization, etc., and contains a warning that any erasures will be penalized. The practice typing helps make sure that the typewriter is functioning properly.

After the 3 minutes' practice typing, instruct the competitors to put fresh paper in their machines, and to turn the test page over and read the test for 2 minutes. After the 2 minutes, they are instructed to start typing the test. Five minutes are allowed for the test proper.

How the Test Is Rated

The exercise must have been typed about once to meet the speed requirement of 40 words a minute. If this speed is not attained, the test is not scored for accuracy. As shown in Exhibit No. 7, a test paper that contains 17 lines meets the minimum speed requirement. Applicants have been instructed to begin and end each line precisely as in the printed test copy. From Exhibit No. 7 it can be quickly determined whether a typing test is to be rated for accuracy and, if so, the greatest number of errors permitted for the lines typed.

The next step is to compare the test paper with the printed test exercise and to mark and charge errors. The basic principles in charging typing errors are as follows:

Charge 1 for each—

WORD or PUNCTUATION MARK incorrectly typed or in which there is an erasure. (An error in spacing which follows an incorrect word or punctuation mark is not further charged.)

SERIES of consecutive words omitted, repeated, inserted, transposed, or erased. Charge for errors within such series, but the total charge cannot exceed the number of words.

LINE or part of line typed over other material, typed with all capitals, or apparently typed with the fingers on the wrong keys.

Change from the MARGIN where most lines are begun by the applicant or from the PARAGRAPH INDENTION most frequently used by the applicant.

The typing score used in the official examination reflects both speed and accuracy, with accuracy weighted twice as heavily as speed. Other methods of rating typing often used in schools are based on gross words per minute or net words per minute (usually with not more than a fixed number of errors). Exhibit No. 8 will enable teachers and applicants to calculate typing proficiency in terms of gross words per minute and errors, and to determine whether that proficiency meets the minimum standards of eligibility required in the regular Civil Service examination.

Exhibit No. 8 gives the maximum number of errors permitted at various speeds for three different levels of typing ability. For example, at the minimum acceptable speed of 17 lines, or 40 gross words per minute, 3 errors are permitted for eligibility as GS–2 Clerk-Typist or GS–3 Clerk-Stenographer. For GS–3 Clerk-Typist and GS–4 Clerk-Stenographer, and for GS–4 Clerk-Typist and GS–5 Clerk-Stenographer, higher standards of accuracy in relation to speed are required.

How To Construct Additional Tests

Here are some of the principal points followed by the examining staff in constructing typing tests so that the various tests will be comparable.

A passage should be subject matter that might reasonably be given a new typist in a Government office. All words must be in sufficiently common use to be understood by most high school seniors, and the more difficult words must be dispersed throughout the passage rather than concentrated in one or two sentences. Sentence structure is not complicated. The length of the test exercise in Exhibit No. 6 is typical—21 lines of about 60 strokes each, with a total of about 1,250 strokes.

STENOGRAPHER-TYPIST EXAMINATION

EXHIBIT NO. 6. COPYING FROM PLAIN COPY

(Part of the Stenographer-Typist Examination)

Read these directions carefully.

A practice exercise appears at the bottom of this sheet, and the test exercise itself is on the back. First study these directions. Then, when the signal is given, begin to practice by typing the practice exercise below on the paper that has been given you. The examiner will tell you when to stop typing the practice exercise.

In both the practice and the test exercises, *space, paragraph, spell, punctuate, capitalize, and begin and end each line* precisely as shown in the exercises.

The examiner will tell you the exact time you will have to make repeated copies of the test exercise. Each time you complete the exercise, simply double space and begin again. If you fill up one side of the paper, turn it over and continue typing on the other side. Keep on typing until told to stop.

Keep in mind that you must meet minimum standards in both speed and accuracy and that, above these standards, accuracy is twice as important as speed. Make no erasures, insertions, or other corrections in this plain-copy test. Since errors are penalized whether or not they are erased or otherwise "corrected," it is best to keep on typing even though you detect an error.

PRACTICE EXERCISE

```
     This practice exercise is similar in form and in diffi-
culty to the one that you will be required to typewrite for
the plain-copy test.  You are to space, capitalize, punctu-
ate, spell, and begin and end each line precisely as in the
copy.  Make no erasures, insertions, or other changes in
this test because errors will be penalized even if they are
erased or otherwise corrected.  Practice typewriting this
material on scratch paper until the examiner tells you to stop,
remembering that for this examination it is more important
for you to typewrite accurately than to typewrite rapidly.
```

TEST EXERCISE

Because they have often learned to know types of architecture by decoration, casual observers sometimes fail to realize that the significant part of a structure is not the ornamentation but the body itself. Architecture, because of its close contact with human lives, is peculiarly and intimately governed by climate. For instance, a home built for comfort in the cold and snow of the northern areas of this country would be unbearably warm in a country with weather such as that of Cuba. A Cuban house, with its open court, would prove impossible to heat in a northern winter.

Since the purpose of architecture is the construction of shelters in which human beings may carry on their numerous activities, the designer must consider not only climatic conditions but also the function of a building. Thus, although the climate of a certain locality requires that an auditorium and a hospital have several features in common, the purposes for which they will be used demand some difference in structure. For centuries builders have first complied with these two requirements and later added whatever ornamentation they wished. Logically, we should see as mere additions, not as basic parts, the details by which we identify architecture.

EACH TIME YOU REACH THIS POINT, DOUBLE SPACE AND BEGIN AGAIN.

EXHIBIT NO. 7. LINE KEY FOR 5-MINUTE TYPING TEST SHOWING MAXIMUM NUMBER OF ERRORS PERMISSIBLE FOR VARIOUS TYPING SPEEDS, AT GRADES GS–2 TYPIST AND GS–3 STENOGRAPHER

Speed.—In the following example, more than 16 lines must have been typed for any speed rating. This sample key is constructed on the premise that if the competitor made the first stroke in her final line (even if it was an error), she is given credit for that line in determining the gross words per minute.

Accuracy.—The gross words per minute typed, at any line, is the number *outside* the parentheses opposite that line. The numbers *in* the parentheses show the maximum number of errors permitted for that number of gross words per minute typed. The number of errors permitted increases with the speed. (This sample key shows the requirements for GS–2 typist and GS–3 stenographer. Exhibit No. 8 shows the standards for higher grades.) If the number of strokes per line were different, this table would have to be altered accordingly.

	Maximum Number of Errors Per Gross Words Per Minute Typed	
	1st typing of exercise	2d typing of exercise
Because they have often learned to know types of archi-	------	52(7)
tecture by decoration, casual observers sometimes fail to	------	54(7)
realize that the significant part of a structure is not the	------	56(8)
ornamentation but the body itself. Architecture, because	------	59(8)
of its close contact with human lives, is peculiarly and	------	61(9)
intimately governed by climate. For instance, a home built	------	64(9)
ior comfort in the cold and snow of the northern areas of	------	66(10)
this country would be unbearably warm in a country with	------	68(10)
weather such as that of Cuba. A Cuban house, with its open	------	71(11)
court, would prove impossible to heat in a northern winter.	------	73(11)
Since the purpose of architecture is the construction of	------	76(12)
shelters in which human beings may carry on their numerous	------	78(12)
activities, the designer must consider not only climatic con-	------	80(12)[2]
ditions, but also the function of a building. Thus, although	------	------
the climate of a certain locality requires that an auditorium	------	------
and a hospital have several features in common, the purposes	------	------
for which they will be used demand some difference in struc-	40(3)[1]	------
ture. For centuries builders have first complied with these	42(4)	------
two requirements and later added whatever ornamentation they	44(5)	------
wished. Logically, we should see as mere additions, not as	47(6)	------
basic parts, the details by which we identify architecture.	49(6)	------

[1] The minimum rated speed is 40 gross words per minute for typing from printed copy.

[2] Any material typed after 80 gross words per minute (which is considered 100 in speed) is *not* rated for accuracy.

Note: The number of errors shown above must be proportionately increased for tests which are longer than 5 minutes.

EXHIBIT NO. 8. MAXIMUM NUMBER OF ERRORS PERMITTED ON 5-MINUTE TESTS AT VARIOUS SPEEDS FOR TYPING SCORES REQUIRED FOR TYPIST AND STENOGRAPHER POSITIONS

SPEED	MAXIMUM NUMBER OF ERRORS PERMITTED		
Gross Words Per Minute	*GS–2 Clerk-Typist GS–3 Clerk-Stenographer*	*GS–3 Clerk-Typist GS–4 Clerk-Stenographer*	*GS–4 Clerk-Typist GS–5 Clerk-Stenographer*
Under 40	Ineligible	Ineligible	Ineligible
40	3	3	2
41–42	4	4	2
43–44	5	4	2
45–47	6	5	3
48–49	6	5	3
50–52	7	6	4
53–54	7	6	4
55–56	8	7	5
57–59	8	7	5
60–61	9	8	6
62–64	9	8	7
65–66	10	9	7
67–68	10	9	8
69–71	11	10	8
72–73	11	10	9
74–76	12	11	10
77–78	12	11	10
79–80	12	12	10

NOTE: THE NUMBER OF ERRORS SHOWN ABOVE MUST BE PROPORTIONATELY INCREASED FOR TESTS WHICH ARE LONGER THAN 5 MINUTES.

The Dictation Test

The dictation test includes a practice dictation and a test exercise, each consisting of 240 words. The rate of dictation is 80 words a minute.

The dictation passages are nontechnical subject matter that might be given a stenographer in a Government office. Sentence structure is not complicated and sentences are not extremely long or short. The words average 1.5 syllables in length.

As shown in Exhibit No. 9, each dictation passage is printed with spacing to show the point that the dictator should reach at the end of each 10 seconds in order to maintain an even dictation rate of 80 words a minute. This indication of timing is one device for assisting all examiners to conform to the intended dictation rate. All examiners are also sent instructions for dictating and a sample passage to be used in practicing dictating before the day of the test. By using these devices for securing uniform dictating and by providing alternate dictation passages that are as nearly equal as possible, the Commission can give each applicant a test that is neither harder nor easier than those given others competing for the same jobs.

The test differs from the conventional dictation test in the method of transcribing the notes. The applicant is not required to type a transcript of the notes, but follows a procedure that permits machine scoring of the test. When typewritten transcripts were still required, examiners rated the test by comparing every word of a competitor's paper with the material dictated and charging errors. Fairness to those competing for employment required that comparable errors be penalized equally. Because of the variety of errors and combinations of errors that can be made in transcripts, the scoring of typewritten transcripts required considerable training and consumed much time—many months for large nationwide examinations. After years of experimentation, a transcript booklet procedure was devised that simplified and speeded the scoring procedure.

Today, rating is decentralized to U.S. Civil Service Commission area offices, and test scores can be furnished quickly and accurately. The transcript booklet makes these improvements possible.

How the Transcript Booklet Works

The transcript booklet (see Exhibit No. 11) gives the stenographer parts of the dictated passage, but leaves blank spaces where many of the words belong. With adequate shorthand notes, the stenographer can readily fit the correct words into the blank spaces, which are numbered 1 through 125. At the left of the printed partial transcript is a list of words, each word with a capital letter A, B, C, or D beside it. Knowing from the notes what word belongs in a blank space, the competitor looks for it among the words in the list. The letter beside the word or phrase in the list is the answer to be marked in the space on the transcript. In the list there are other words that a competitor with inadequate notes might guess belong in that space, but the capital letter beside these words would be an incorrect answer. (Some persons find it helpful to write the word or the shorthand symbol in the blank space before looking for it in the word list. There is no objection to doing this.)

Look, for example, at the Practice Dictation Transcript Sheet, Exhibit No. 10, question 10. The word dictated is "physical"; it is in the word list with a capital "D." In the transcript, blank number 10 should be answered "D."

None of the words in the list is marked "E." This is because the answer "E" is reserved for any question when the word dictated for that spot does not appear in the list. Every transcript booklet has spots for which the list does not include the correct words. This provision reduces the possibility that competitors may guess correct answers.

After the stenographer has written the letter of the missing word or phrase in each numbered blank of the transcript, he transfers the answers to the proper spaces on the answer sheet. Directions for marking the separate answer sheet are given on page 1 of Exhibit No. 11.

This transcription procedure should not cause any good stenographer to make a poor showing on the examination. To this end, illustrations of the procedure are included in a sheet of samples that is mailed to each applicant with the notice of when and where to report for examination. Again in the examination room, the applicant uses such a transcript on the practice dictation before the actual dictation is given. A major objective in preparing this publication is to further insure that each prospective competitor is made to feel at ease about using this method of indicating how good the notes are.

Use of the transcript booklet and transfer of answers to the answer sheet are clerical tasks that are not part of transcribing by typewriter. Most stenographic positions involve clerical duties for some percentage of the time and it is reasonable, therefore, to include clerical tasks in the examination. Although some unsuccessful competitors for stenographic positions attribute their failure to the use of transcript booklets, analysis of many test papers, notes, and transcripts has shown the frequency of clerical error in this test to be negligible.

How the Test Is Administered

Each competitor will need a copy of the Practice Dictation Transcript Sheet (Exhibit No. 10), a copy of the Transcript Booklet (Exhibit No. 11), and an answer sheet (Exhibit No. 2). These should be distributed at the times indicated below.

The Practice Dictation of Exhibit No. 9 should be dictated at the rate indicated by the 10-second divisions in which it is printed. This will be at the rate of 80 words a minute. Then each competitor should be given a copy of the Practice Dictation Transcript Sheet and allowed 7 minutes to study the instructions and to transcribe part of the practice dictation.

The test exercise (reverse of Exhibit No. 9) should also be dictated at the rate of 80 words a minute, for 3 minutes. Each competitor should be given a Transcript Booklet and an answer sheet. He should be told that he will have 3 minutes for reading the directions on the face page, followed by 30 minutes for writing answers in the blank spaces, and then 10 minutes for transferring his answers to the answer sheet. These time limits are those used in the official examination and have been found ample.

How the Answer Sheet Is Scored

The correct answers for the test are given in Exhibit No. 12. A scoring stencil may be prepared by copying these answers on a blank answer sheet and then punching out the marked answer boxes. Directions for using the scoring stencil are given at the top of Exhibit No. 12.

In some rare instances where the typewritten transcript is still used, the passing standard on the total transcript is 24 or fewer errors for GS–3 Clerk-Stenographer, and 12 or fewer errors for GS–4. Comparable standards on the parts of the dictation measured by the machine-scored method of transcription are 14 or fewer errors for GS–3, and 6 or fewer errors for GS–4 positions.

A stenographer who can take dictation at 80 words a minute with this degree of accuracy is considered fully qualified. Positions such as Reporting Stenographer and Shorthand Reporter require ability to take dictation at much higher speeds. The test for Reporting Stenographer is dictated at 120 words a minute. Two rates of dictation, 160 and 175 words a minute, are used for the Shorthand Reporter tests for different grade levels.

How To Construct Additional Tests

A teacher who has examined students by the tests in this part may wish to reexamine some of them after a period of further training. For this purpose it is desirable to use new tests rather than to repeat the same test too often. If additional test material is needed, it should be constructed in accordance with the following principles in order to keep alternative tests comparable.

As already indicated, the subject matter and the vocabulary should not be technical or too unusual; they should appear to be part of the day-to-day business of an efficient Government office. In view of the broad range of activities of Federal agencies, this restriction still allows a wide range of subject matter.

For 3 minutes of dictation at 80 words a minute, the exercise should contain 240 words. The average number of syllables should be about 1.5. Sentences should be straightforward, rather than of complicated grammatical construction. At the same time, they should not be short and choppy.

Before the transcript booklet is made, a skeleton transcript should be prepared. One way of beginning is to choose words and groups of words that should be tested. A total of about 140 words of the complete dictation passage should be chosen for testing, since some of the 125 numbered blank spaces in the transcript booklet should represent more than one word. As shown in the transcripts in Exhibits No. 10 and 11, the words selected for testing are not chosen simply by taking every other word; rather, they are single words or series of words distributed throughout the dictation passage. The first word of any sentence should not be used as a test word.

The dictation passage should be divided into four sections of about equal length with a section always breaking at the end of a sentence. A worksheet similar to that shown below should be prepared for each section.

For illustration of the next steps, look at the reverse side of the Practice Dictation Transcript Sheet, Exhibit No. 10; let the two sentences at the bottom of that page represent the dictation. The words that have been chosen for testing are "bring," "about," "to visit," "their," "to discuss," "treatment," "correction," and so on; these words or phrases have been numbered 16, 17, etc. For a convenient worksheet, ruled paper can be divided into columns headed A, B, C, D, and E. Now the words chosen for the blanks should be distributed at random in the various columns. At this point the worksheet for this part of the test will look like this:

	A	B	C	D	E
16	bring				
17					about
18		to visit			
19				their	
20				to discuss	
21					treatment
22			correction		
23					value
24		see			
25	is not				

(and so on.)

Next, think of several plausible errors for each of the blanks; that is, a word beginning with the same sound, a word that fits the preceding or the following word almost as a cliché, etc. Avoid any error that is too conspicuously wrong or too clearly a misfit with printed auxiliaries or articles to present any difficulty. Place each plausible error in column A, B, C, or D of the worksheet, *avoiding* the column that contains the *answer*. The worksheet will now look like the columns below.

Experience will bring out situations that must be avoided, such as use of the same word in more than one column.

Each word in columns A, B, C, and D takes the letter at the head of the column. The words in these columns are grouped in alphabetic order to become the "Word List" for the section of the transcript covered by this worksheet. Since instructions provide that E is to be selected when the exact answer is not listed, the words in column E are NOT included in the "Word List." The sentences are presented with numbered blanks as the "Transcript."

	A	B	C	D	E
16	<u>bring</u>	promote	discuss	understand	
17	all				<u>about</u>
18	visit	<u>to visit</u>	at	during	
19	(all)		young	<u>their</u>	
20	to discover	undertake	to endorse indicated	<u>to discuss</u>	
21	treatments				<u>treatment</u>
22	reducing	collection	<u>correction</u>	recognizing	
23	friend	volume		virtue	<u>value</u>
24	know	<u>see</u>	say	satisfied	
25	<u>is not</u>	is	soon	knows insisted	

(and so on.)

EXHIBIT NO. 9. DICTATION TEST

(Part of the Stenographer-Typist Examination)

PRACTICE DICTATION

INSTRUCTIONS TO THE EXAMINER: This Practice Dictation and one exercise will be dictated at the rate of 80 words a minute. Do not dictate the punctuation except for periods, but dictate with the expression that the punctuation indicates. Use a watch with a second hand to enable you to read the exercises at the proper speed.

Exactly on a minute, start dictating.

	Finish reading each two lines at the number of seconds indicated below
I realize that this practice dictation is not a part of the examination	**10**
proper and is not to be scored. (Period) The work of preventing and correcting	**20**
physical defects in children is becoming more effective as a result of a change	**30**
in the attitude of many parents. (Period) In order to bring about this change,	**40**
mothers have been invited to visit the schools when their children are being examined	**50**
and to discuss the treatment necessary for the correction of defects. (Period)	**1 min.**
There is a distinct value in having a mother see that her child is not the	**10**
only one who needs attention. (Period) Otherwise a few parents might feel that they	**20**
were being criticized by having the defects of their children singled out for medical	**30**
treatment. (Period) The special classes that have been set up have shown the value of	**40**
the scientific knowledge that has been applied in the treatment of children. (Period)	**50**
In these classes the children have been taught to exercise by a trained teacher	**2 min.**
under medical supervision. (Period) The hours of the school day have been divided	**10**
between school work and physical activity that helps not only to correct their defects	**20**
but also to improve their general physical condition. (Period) This method of treatment	**30**
has been found to be very effective except for those who have severe medical	**40**
defects. (Period) Most parents now see how desirable it is to have these classes	**50**
that have been set up in the regular school system to meet special needs. (Period)	**3 min.**

After dictating the practice, pause for 15 seconds to permit competitors to complete their notes. Then continue in accordance with the directions for conducting the examination.

After the Practice Dictation Transcript has been completed, dictate the test from the reverse of this card.

(OVER)

EXHIBIT NO. 9—continued.

(See reverse for Practice Dictation.)

Exactly on a minute, start dictating.

	Finish reading each two lines at the number of seconds indicated below
The number enrolled in shorthand classes in the high schools has shown a marked increase. (Period)	10
Today this subject is one of the most popular offered in the field of	20
business education. (Period) When shorthand was first taught, educators claimed that it was of	30
value mainly in sharpening the powers of observation and discrimination. (Period)	40
However, with the growth of business and the increased demand for office workers,	50
educators have come to realize the importance of stenography as a vocational	1 min.
tool. (Period) With the differences in the aims of instruction came changes in	10
the grade placement of the subject. (Period) The prevailing thought has always been that it	20
should be offered in high school. (Period) When the junior high school first came into	30
being, shorthand was moved down to that level with little change in the manner in which	40
the subject was taught. (Period) It was soon realized that shorthand had no place there	50
because the training had lost its vocational utility by the time the student could	2 min.
graduate. (Period) Moreover, surveys of those with education only through junior	10
high school seldom found them at work as stenographers. (Period) For this reason, shorthand	20
was returned to the high school level and is offered as near as possible to the time	30
of graduation so that the skill will be retained when the student takes a job. (Period)	40
Because the age at which students enter office jobs has advanced, there is now	50
a tendency to upgrade business education into the junior college. (Period)	3 min.

After completing the dictation, pause for 15 seconds.

Give a Transcript to each competitor.

EXHIBIT NO. 10. PRACTICE DICTATION TRANSCRIPT SHEET

(Part of the Stenographer-Typist Examination)

The TRANSCRIPT below is part of the material that was dictated to you for practice, except that many of the words have been left out. From your notes, you are to tell what the missing words are. Proceed as follows:

Compare your notes with the TRANSCRIPT and, when you come to a blank in the TRANSCRIPT, decide what word or words belong there. For example, you will find that the word "practice" belongs in blank number 1. Look at the WORD LIST to see whether you can find the same word there. Notice what letter (A, B, C, or D) is printed beside it, and write that letter in the blank. For example, the word "practice" is listed, followed by the letter "B." We have already written "B" in blank number 1 to show you how you are to record your choice. Now decide what belongs in each of the other blanks. (You may also write the word or words, or the shorthand for them, if you wish.) The same word may belong in more than one blank. If the exact answer is not listed, write "E" in the blank.

ALPHABETIC WORD LIST

about—B
against—C
attitude—A
being—D
childhood—B
children—A
correcting—C
doctors—B
effective—D
efficient—A
examination—A
examining—C
for—B
health—B
mothers—C
never—C
not—D
paper—B
parents—B
part—C
physical—D
portion—D
practical—A
practice—B
preliminary—D
preventing—B
procedure—A
proper—C
reason for—A
result—B
result of—C
schools—C
to be—C
to prevent—A

TRANSCRIPT

I realize that this B (1) dictation is ____ (2) a ____ (3) of the ____ (4) ____ (5) and is ____ (6) ____ (7) scored.

The work of ____ (8) and ____ (9) ____ (10) defects in ____ (11) is becoming more ____ (12) as a ____ (13) a change in the ____ (14) of many ____ (15). . . .

Sample Answer Sheet

	A	B	C	D	E
1	▯	▮	▯	▯	▯
2	▯	▯	▯	▯	▯
3	▯	▯	▯	▯	▯
4	▯	▯	▯	▯	▯
5	▯	▯	▯	▯	▯
6	▯	▯	▯	▯	▯
7	▯	▯	▯	▯	▯
8	▯	▯	▯	▯	▯

Each numbered blank in the TRANSCRIPT is a question. You will be given a separate answer sheet like the sample here, to which you will transfer your answers. The answer sheet has a numbered row of boxes for each question. The answer for blank number 1 is "B." We have already transferred this to number 1 in the Sample Answer Sheet, by darkening the box under "B."

Now transfer your answer for each of questions 2 through 15 to the answer sheet. That is, beside each number on the answer sheet find the letter that is the same as the letter you wrote in the blank with the same number in the TRANSCRIPT, and darken the box below that letter.

After you have marked 15, continue with blank number 16 on the back of this sheet **WITHOUT WAITING FOR A SIGNAL.**

Sample Answer Sheet (Continued)

	A	B	C	D	E
9	▯	▯	▯	▯	▯
10	▯	▯	▯	▯	▯
11	▯	▯	▯	▯	▯
12	▯	▯	▯	▯	▯
13	▯	▯	▯	▯	▯
14	▯	▯	▯	▯	▯
15	▯	▯	▯	▯	▯

EXHIBIT NO. 10—continued.

WORD LIST

Write *E* if the answer is NOT listed.

all—A	reducing—A
at—C	satisfied—D
bring—A	say—C
collection—B	see—B
correction—C	soon—C
discuss—C	their—D
during—D	to discover—A
friend—A	to discuss—D
indicated—C	to endorse—C
insisted—D	to visit—B
is—B	treatments—A
is not—A	understand—D
know—A	undertake—B
knows—D	virtue—D
needed—B	visit—A
promote—B	volume—B
recognizing—D	young—C

TRANSCRIPT (continued)

. . . In order to .... (16) .... (17) this change, mothers have been invited .... (18) the schools when .... (19) children are being examined and .... (20) the .... (21) necessary for the .... (22) of defects. There is a distinct .... (23) in having a mother .... (24) that her child .... (25) the only one who needs attention. . . .

(The rest of the practice dictation is not transcribed here.)

Sample Answer Sheet (Continued)

	A	B	C	D	E
16	▯	▯	▯	▯	▯
17	▯	▯	▯	▯	▯
18	▯	▯	▯	▯	▯
19	▯	▯	▯	▯	▯
20	▯	▯	▯	▯	▯
21	▯	▯	▯	▯	▯
22	▯	▯	▯	▯	▯
23	▯	▯	▯	▯	▯
24	▯	▯	▯	▯	▯
25	▯	▯	▯	▯	▯

Your notes should show that the word "bring" goes in blank 16, and "about" in blank 17. But "about" is *not in the list;* so "E" should be your answer for question 17.

The two words, "to visit—B," are needed for 18, and the one word "visit—A," would be an incorrect answer.

Fold this page so that the Correct Answers to Samples 1 through 8, below, will lie beside the Sample Answer Sheet you marked for those questions. Compare your answers with the correct answers. Then fold the page and compare the correct answers with your answers for 9 through 15. If one of your answers does not agree with the correct answer, again compare your notes with the samples and make certain you understand the instructions. The correct answers for 16 through 25 are as follows: 16 A; 17 E; 18 B; 19 D; 20 D; 21 E; 22 C; 23 E; 24 B; and 25 A.

For the actual test you will use a separate answer sheet. As scoring will be done by an electronic scoring machine, it is important that you follow directions carefully. Use a medium No. 2 pencil. You must keep your mark for a question within the box. If you have to erase a mark, be sure to erase it completely. Mark only one answer for each question.

Correct Answers to Sample Questions 1 through 8

	A	B	C	D	E
1	▯	▮	▯	▯	▯
2	▯	▯	▯	▮	▯
3	▯	▯	▮	▯	▯
4	▮	▯	▯	▯	▯
5	▯	▯	▮	▯	▯
6	▯	▯	▯	▮	▯
7	▯	▯	▮	▯	▯
8	▯	▮	▯	▯	▯

For any stenographer who missed the practice dictation, part of it is given below:

"I realize that this practice dictation is not a part of the examination proper and is not to be scored.

"The work of preventing and correcting physical defects in children is becoming more effective as a result of a change in the attitude of many parents. In order to bring about this change, mothers have been invited to visit the schools when their children are being examined and to discuss the treatment necessary for the correction of defects. There is a distinct value in having a mother see that her child is not the only one who needs attention. . . ."

Correct Answers to Sample Questions 9 through 15

	A	B	C	D	E
9	▯	▯	▮	▯	▯
10	▯	▯	▯	▮	▯
11	▮	▯	▯	▯	▯
12	▯	▯	▯	▮	▯
13	▯	▯	▮	▯	▯
14	▮	▯	▯	▯	▯
15	▯	▮	▯	▯	▯

(Page 2 of Exhibit No. 10)

EXHIBIT NO. 11. TRANSCRIPT BOOKLET—DICTATION TEST

(Part of Stenographer-Typist Examination)

Directions for Completing the TRANSCRIPT

A TRANSCRIPT of the dictation you have just taken is given on pages 14 & 15. As in the TRANSCRIPT for the practice dictation, there are numbered blank spaces for many of the words that were dictated. You are to compare your notes with the TRANSCRIPT and, when you come to a blank, decide what word or words belong there. For most of the blanks the words are included in the list beside the TRANSCRIPT; each is followed by a letter, A, B, C, or D. To show that you know which word or words belong in each blank space, you are to *write the letter* in the blank. You are to write E if the exact answer is NOT listed. (In addition you may write the word or words, or the shorthand for them, if you wish.) The same choice may belong in more than one blank.

After you have compared your notes with the TRANSCRIPT and have chosen the answer for each blank space, you will be given additional time to transfer your answers to a separate answer sheet.

Directions for Marking the Separate Answer Sheet

On the answer sheet, each question number stands for the blank with the same number in the TRANSCRIPT. For each number, you are to darken the box below the letter that is the same as the letter you wrote in the TRANSCRIPT. (The answers in this booklet will not be rated.) Be sure to use your pencil and record your answers on the separate answer sheet. You must keep your mark within the box. If you have to erase a mark, be sure to erase it completely. Make only one mark for each question.

Work quickly so that you will be able to finish in the time allowed. First you should darken the boxes on the answer sheet for the blanks you have lettered. You may continue to use your notes if you have not finished writing letters in the blanks in the TRANSCRIPT, or if you wish to make sure you have lettered them correctly.

DO NOT OPEN THIS BOOKLET UNTIL TOLD TO DO SO.

WORD LIST

Write *E* if the answer is NOT listed.

administration—C
along the—B
area—A
at first—A
claimed—C
classes—B
concluded—D
could be—D
courses—C
decrease—D
discriminating—C
discrimination—D
education—B
enrolled—D
entering—A
field—D
first—D
given—B
great—C
increase—A
in the—D
known—D
line—C
mainly—B
marked—B
mostly—D

observation—B
observing—A
offered—C
of value—C
open—A
popular—B
power—B
powers—D
practical—A
shaping—A
sharpen—B
shorthand—D
shown—C
stenography—B
study—C
subject—A
taught—D
that—C
the—D
these—B
this—A
thought—B
to be—A
training—D
valuable—A
vast—A

TRANSCRIPT

The number ....(1) in shorthand ....(2) ....(3) high schools has ....(4) a ....(5) ....(6). Today ....(7) ....(8) is one of the most ....(9) ....(10) ....(11) ....(12) of business ....(13). When ....(14) ....(15) ....(16) ....(17), educators ....(18) that it ....(19) ....(20) ....(21) in ....(22) ....(23) ....(24) of ....(25) and ....(26). . . .

WORD LIST

Write *E* if the answer is NOT listed.

a change—D
administration—C
aims—A
always been—A
begun—D
businesses—A
came—D
changes—B
come—C
defects—B
demand—B
demands—A
differences—D
education—B
educators—D
for—D
given—B
grade—C
grading—B
has—C
had—B
have come—A
high school—B
increased—D
increasing—C
institutions—D
instruction—C
it—B

offered—C
office—A
official—C
often been—B
ought to be—B
place—B
placement—D
prevailing—B
rule—D
schools—D
shorthand—D
should be—A
significance—C
stenography—B
study—C
subject—A
thinking—C
this—A
thought—B
tool—B
to realize—B
to recognize—B
valuable—A
vocational—C
when the—D
with—A
without—C
workers—C

TRANSCRIPT (continued)

. . . However, ...(27) the growth of ....(28) and the ....(29) ....(30) for ....(31) ....(32), ...(33) have ....(34) ....(35) the ....(36) of ....(37) ....(38) a ....(39) ....(40). With the ....(41) in the ....(42) of ....(43) ....(44) ....(45) in the ....(46) ....(47) of the ....(48). The ....(49) ....(50) ....(51) ....(52) that ....(53) ....(54) ....(55) in ....(56). . . .

CONTINUE ON THE NEXT PAGE WITHOUT WAITING FOR A SIGNAL.

(Page 2 of Exhibit No. 11)

WORD LIST

Write *E* if the answer is NOT listed.

became—B
because—B
came—D
change—A
changed—C
could—C
could be—D
date—D
first—D
graduate—D
graduated—B
had little—C
had no—A
here—D
high—C
into being—A
into business—C
junior high—D
less—B
lessened—C
level—C
little—A
lost—D
manner—B
method—C

moved—C
moved down—B
occupational—B
recognized—A
shorthand—D
since—C
soon—C
stenography—B
student—A
students—C
study—C
subject—A
taught—D
that—C
the—D
their—B
there—B
this—A
time—B
training—D
usefulness—B
utility—C
vocational—C
which—A

TRANSCRIPT (continued)

. . . When the .... school ...., ...
57 58 59 60 61

was .... to .... with .... in ....
62 63 64 65 66 67 68

.... the .... was .... It was .... that ....
69 70 71 72 73 74

.... place .... the .... had ....
75 76 77 78 79 80 81

.... by the .... the ....
82 83 84 85 86

WORD LIST

Write *E* if the answer is NOT listed.

advanced—A
age—A
as far as—C
at which—D
at work—A
be—B
date—D
education—B
enter—D
found—D
graduating—A
graduation—C
has—C
high school—B
in—A
in order—D
increased—D
into—B
job—B
junior high—D
level—C
may be—C
near as—A
nearly as—C
offered—C
often—B
only—B
possible—D

rarely—D
reason—B
reasons—D
retained—B
school—A
secretaries—D
secures—D
seldom—C
showed—A
so—A
stenographers—C
studies—B
surveys—A
takes—A
taught—D
tendency—B
that—C
there—B
this—A
through—D
time—B
training—D
undertake—A
until—A
upgrade—D
when—C
which—A
will—B
would—D
working—B

TRANSCRIPT (continued)

. . . Moreover, ... of .... with ....
87 88 89 90 91

.... school .... them .... as .... For ....
92 93 94 95 96 97

......., shorthand was .... to the .... and is ....
98 99 100 101 102

as .... to the .... of .... the skill
103 104 105 106 107 108

.... the student .... a ....
109 110 111 112 113 114

Because the .... students .... office ....
115 116 117 118 119

......., there is .... a .... to .... education ....
120 121 122 123 124 125

the junior college.

(Page 3 of Exhibit No. 11)

KEY (CORRECT ANSWERS)

EXHIBIT NO. 12. SCORING STENCIL—RIGHT ANSWERS

Dictation Test

If the competitor marked more than one answer to any question, draw a line through the answer boxes for the question. To make a stencil, punch out the answers on this page or on a separate answer sheet. Place this punched key over a competitor's sheet. Count the right answers. DO NOT GIVE CREDIT FOR DOUBLE ANSWERS.

1	D	26	D	51	C	76	B	101	C
2	B	27	A	52	A	77	B	102	C
3	D	28	E	53	B	78	D	103	A
4	C	29	D	54	A	79	D	104	D
5	B	30	B	55	C	80	E	105	B
6	A	31	A	56	B	81	C	106	C
7	A	32	C	57	D	82	C	107	A
8	A	33	D	58	D	83	B	108	C
9	B	34	C	59	D	84	A	109	B
10	C	35	B	60	A	85	C	110	B

Make only ONE mark for each answer. Additional and stray marks may be counted as mistakes. In making corrections, erase errors COMPLETELY.

11	D	36	E	61	D	86	D	111	B
12	D	37	B	62	B	87	A	112	C
13	B	38	E	63	C	88	E	113	A
14	D	39	C	64	C	89	B	114	B
15	E	40	B	65	A	90	B	115	A
16	D	41	D	66	A	91	D	116	D
17	D	42	A	67	D	92	D	117	D
18	C	43	C	68	B	93	C	118	E
19	E	44	D	69	E	94	D	119	C
20	C	45	B	70	A	95	A	120	A
21	B	46	C	71	D	96	C	121	E
22	E	47	[illegible]	72	[illegible]	97	[illegible]	122	B
23	D	48	A	73	[illegible]	98	B	123	D
24	D	49	B	74	[illegible]	99	E	124	E
25	B	50	B	75	A	100	B	125	B